DESTINY'S DOGS

Georgia's Championship Season

By
Mark Schlabach
and
The Atlanta Journal-Constitution
Photography Staff

The Atlanta
Journal-
Constitution
ajc.com

SP
SPORTS
PUBLISHING
L.L.C.

www.sportspublishingllc.com

Publisher
PETER L. BANNON

Senior Managing Editors
SUSAN M. MOYER AND
JOSEPH J. BANNON, JR.

Coordinating Editor
NOAH ADAMS AMSTADTER

Art Director
K. JEFFREY HIGGERSON

Interior Design
TRACY GAUDREAU

Cover Design
KENNETH J. O'BRIEN

Book Layout
JENNIFER L. POLSON

Imaging
KERRI BAKER, KENNETH J. O'BRIEN AND
CHRISTINE MOHRBACHER

Copy Editor
CYNTHIA L. MCNEW

TheAtlanta Journal-Constitution
ajc.com

Publisher
ROGER S. KINTZEL

Editor
JULIA WALLACE

Managing Editors
HANK KLIBANOFF AND
JAMES MALLORY

Deputy Managing Editor/Sports
DON BOYKIN

Sports Editor
ROBERT MASHBURN

Editorial Director/ajc.com
HYDE POST

Assistant Managing Editor/Photography
JOHN GLENN

Director/Information Services
GINNY EVERETT

Front Cover Photo: Curtis Compton/AJC
Back Cover Photo: Brant Sanderlin/AJC

ISBN: 1-58261-691-4

AUTHOR'S NOTE

Dear Friends:

When *The Atlanta Journal-Constitution* published its preseason college football section in August, I got more than a few laughs when I predicted Georgia to finish 12-1 and win its first Southeastern Conference championship in 20 years.

Even my wife, Heather, said I'd lost my mind.

"Georgia's never going to beat Florida," she said. "You're going to look so stupid."

As always, she was right. The Bulldogs again lost to the Gators in Jacksonville, but Georgia beat everybody else. The Bulldogs finished 13-1, including victories over Arkansas in the SEC championship game and Florida State in the Sugar Bowl on New Year's Day.

What did I see in the preseason that made me think the Bulldogs had a chance? Georgia was loaded with talented players, including five seniors on the offensive line. Quarterback David Greene had improved from his rookie season, in which he was named SEC Freshman of the Year. Receivers Terrence Edwards, Damien Gary and Fred Gibson are among the nation's best, and I thought tailback Musa Smith would run for 1,000 yards if he stayed healthy. More than anything, though, Georgia's defense looked fast and the special teams were, well, special.

And the stars seemed to be aligned for the Bulldogs. Florida lost its "Evil Genius" when coach Steve Spurrier left for the NFL. Alabama was on NCAA probation and ineligible to play in the postseason, and LSU and Tennessee lost a lot of talented players to the NFL draft. I figured if Georgia was ever going to win the SEC again, this would have to be the season.

But early in the season, I was starting to have second thoughts about my prediction. The Bulldogs barely beat Clemson in the opener and then needed a miracle to win at South Carolina. With Georgia's offense struggling mightily in the first four games, a victory at Alabama seemed unlikely. But the Bulldogs proved their "manhood" in Tuscaloosa and then won their next three games to set up a showdown against the Gators.

Unfortunately for Georgia fans, Florida handled the Bulldogs 20-13.

Things might have been different if Georgia had been healthy, but the Bulldogs had plenty of chances to win that game nonetheless. With their backs against the wall the next two weeks, the Bulldogs did something that so many previous Georgia teams had failed to do — they won games when they had to win.

Needing to win their last two games to claim the SEC's East Division, the Bulldogs more than handled Ole Miss in Athens, and then won on a miracle play at Auburn. After that, everything came easy. Georgia crushed rival Georgia Tech and whipped the Razorbacks in the Georgia Dome.

Finally, the drought was over.

After 20 years of frustration, Georgia fans will want to relive the 2002 season for years to come. Hopefully, this book will give you the chance to do just that. We've documented the Bulldogs' memorable season with game stories and profiles and images from the *Journal-Constitution's* award-winning photography staff.

Enjoy.

Mark Schlabach

Mark Schlabach

Georgia 24, Auburn 21

Fourth & Fabulous!

Greene-to-Johnson TD: 'It was a beautiful ball'

The coach · The quarterback · The receiver · 'He just outjumped us'

The Atlanta Journal-Constitution — college football

2002 SEC EAST Champions!

Destiny's Dogs

SPORTS — GEORGIA 51, GEORGIA TECH 7

Call off the Dogs!

Richt's stamp is the difference in Georgia

'Greatest game Falcons ever played'

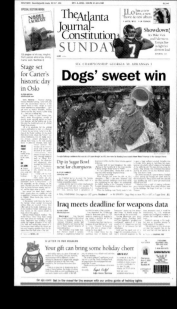

The Atlanta Journal-Constitution — SUNDAY

Dogs' sweet win

Iraq meets deadline for weapons data

sec championship game — 1982 . . . to 2002

Glory, Glory!

Blocked punt releases a roar · Dogs finally end title drought 30-3

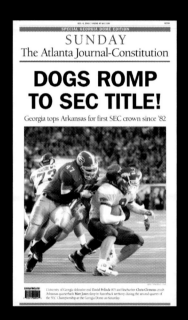

SPECIAL GEORGIA DOME EDITION
SUNDAY — The Atlanta Journal-Constitution

DOGS ROMP TO SEC TITLE!

Georgia tops Arkansas for first SEC crown since '82

the road to glory

Champs at last

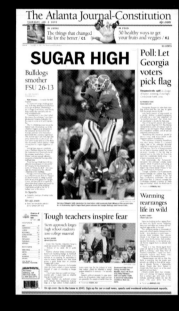

The Atlanta Journal-Constitution

SUGAR HIGH

Bulldogs smother FSU 26-13

Poll: Let Georgia voters pick flag

Tough teachers inspire fear

SPORTS — SUGAR BOWL: GEORGIA 26, FLORIDA STATE 13

Thornton picks up slack

SWEET!

Richt's Dogs first to 13 wins

Deal of infamy: When Falcons lost Favre

Georgia 26, Florida State 13

CATCH IT!

Perfect passes. Timely interceptions. Souvenir beads. Bulldog fever.

Georgia 26, Florida State 13

PARTY TIME!

The Bulldogs cut loose in the Superdome for a Sugar Bowl celebration.

The Atlanta Journal-Constitution
ajc.com

MONDAY, AUGUST 26, 2002

GEORGIA BULLDOGS

FINISH THE DRILL

Richt planted the seeds of a champion with a simple motto

It started with three words.

"Finish the drill."

That was the slogan coach Mark Richt and his assistants started drilling into their players two years ago. Finish the drill, Richt constantly preached, and his players started believing.

From the mat drills at 4:45 a.m. during the offseason to the "Dawg Walk" before games, Richt tried to instill in his players things different and new. He wanted his players to believe they were champions, when maybe nobody else thought they were.

It had been 20 years since the Bulldogs had last won a Southeastern Conference championship. Ronald Reagan was in the White House. Richt was in his last year of college. The Internet and some of Georgia's players hadn't even been born yet.

Twenty years.

"That's a long time. That's a lot of disappointment," Richt said. "It really didn't dawn on me that it was 20 years until the beginning of the season. I was shocked. I told our players, 'Let's change this. Let's knock the lid off this program.'"

And the Bulldogs did. They won where other Georgia teams had annually failed — at

ABOVE:
Mark Richt wanted his players to believe they were champions when maybe nobody else thought they were. John Bazemore, AP/Wide World Photos

South Carolina, Alabama and Auburn. They handed Georgia Tech the worst loss in the history of the 95-year series, and the team that seemingly always lost the close games started winning them. Georgia won five games by six points or less. The Bulldogs needed a gutsy call in the fourth quarter to squeak by Clemson in the opener and then beat the Gamecocks without scoring an offensive touchdown.

But in the SEC championship game, the Bulldogs blasted Arkansas from the opening kickoff, winning 30-3 in Atlanta's Georgia Dome. The Bulldogs won 13 games for the first time and put together a season that can be matched only by the 1980 team that finished 12-0 and won the national championship.

"This goes back to mat drills," junior receiver Damien Gary said. "The coaches are always saying, 'Finish the drill,' and that's what we wanted to do — finish the drill, no matter what."

Mat drills are the offseason conditioning program that Bulldogs strength coach Dave Van Halanger brought from Florida State. He persuaded grown men to roll around on

ABOVE:
In addition to getting the Bulldogs back on track on the field, Mark Richt cleaned up the players' acts off the field.
Jenni Girtman/AJC

mats for four quarters, lasting 15 minutes each — the same as a football game.

"People don't realize what we go through in mat drills," sophomore defensive end David Pollack said. "We get up at 4:45 in the morning, we're pushing each other around on the mats, and your legs feel like Jell-O. Our slogan isn't corny at all. I believe it's coming true."

"'Finish the drill' says to us that, no matter what happens, no matter how you're feeling, you can't get down," senior linebacker Tony Gilbert said. "You push yourself to the limit and then you push yourself a little further."

And it was the seed in building champions.

"The way you build unity is to work guys hard together," Richt said. "When guys work together, it's very difficult to quit. They think, 'I went through all that to get to this.' It teaches you to strain when you're tired, to not give in to circumstances."

The Bulldogs had plenty of chances to quit this season. They came within an eyelash of losing at South Carolina, only winning when Gamecocks running back Andrew Pinnock fumbled inside the Bulldogs' 5-yard line in the final seconds. At Alabama, Georgia blew a 12-point lead and fell behind in the fourth quarter, but the Bulldogs rallied in the closing minutes. At Auburn, it took an improbable touchdown catch from an unlikely hero — on fourth-and-15 with 85 seconds left, no less.

"This team had the intangibles that it takes to be champions," said Georgia athletics director Vince Dooley, who coached the Bulldogs to their last SEC championship in 1982. "They were unified, they played hard and developed as a team."

Indeed, in just his second season at Georgia, Richt pushed the Bulldogs to where they had not been in two decades.

"This is just the start," sophomore receiver Fred Gibson said. "This lets everybody know that the Bulldogs are back and we're for real. We're going to be back here next year and the year after and the year after. The sky is the limit for this program now."

Finally, the Bulldogs are beginning to look toward their future, instead of their past.

"We don't have to hear about 1980 or 1982 anymore," senior linebacker Boss Bailey said. "Now, we get to hear about the 2002 Georgia Bulldogs."

ABOVE:
Many onlookers questioned how effective Georgia would
be with a two-quarterback system featuring sophomore
David Greene and redshirt freshman D.J. Shockley (above),
but their different styles kept Bulldogs opponents guessing.
Jenni Girtman/AJC

SATURDAY, AUGUST 31, 2002
GEORGIA 31, CLEMSON 28

WHEW! DOGS SURVIVE OPENER VS. CLEMSON

Shockley shines at quarterback in Georgia debut

ATHENS, Ga. — All the preseason noise about Georgia's return to football glory came down to one play.

Facing fourth-and-1 at the Georgia 38-yard line with 40 seconds left, Bulldogs coach Mark Richt pondered what to do. His team led 31-28 over Clemson, and conventional wisdom was to punt and try to pin the Tigers deep in their own territory. It was certainly the safe thing to do, after Richt spent much of the offseason being criticized for his late-game clock management last season.

Instead of taking the conventional route, Richt decided to go for it.

No guts, no glory.

Quarterback David Greene took the snap from center, turned and handed off to tailback Musa Smith. Smith plunged over the line for 2 yards and the game-clinching first down.

And just like that, Georgia had won its season opener. Still, many Georgia fans left the stadium shaking their heads, wondering what in the world their coach was thinking.

"We didn't know if we were going to get it, but Coach was like 'Let's go for it,'" Smith said. "The line got a good push, and I just jumped over the top."

Richt said he didn't ponder the decision for very long on the sideline.

"From my vantage point, it looked like about 10 inches," he said. "That's what it looked like to me. For one thing, we had a couple of timeouts. I probably would have punted if we were out of timeouts. But I was like, 'Let's take a timeout and talk about this.' My gut reaction was to punt. I just felt confident that we could get about 10 inches. If we didn't make it, the game was not over."

But if the Bulldogs had failed to gain the first down, Clemson would have had the ball around Georgia's 38-yard line, needing only a couple

BELOW:
Damien Gary's 40-yard punt return set up a touchdown that tied the game at 28 with 12 minutes, 35 seconds left in the fourth quarter. Brant Sanderlin/AJC

ABOVE:
In his regular-season debut for the Bulldogs, redshirt freshman D.J. Shockley ran for a touchdown in the second quarter and threw for one in the fourth.
Brant Sanderlin/AJC

ABOVE:

David Pollack had five tackles and one sack during the Clemson game. He finished the season with 14, a Georgia single-season sacks record. Brant Sanderlin/AJC

of first downs to potentially tie the game with a late field goal.

"Of course, we could have punted," Richt said. "They were out of timeouts, but a punt could get blocked or returned. They may have had a long way to go with 30 seconds left or they could have been in range for a field goal. We happen to have put that play in late in camp. We were thinking of it as a goal-line play that would be a fourth-and-1 to win the game. We just thought it would be at the goal line and not in the middle of the field."

Early in the game, it sure didn't seem like Georgia would need a first down late in the fourth quarter. The Bulldogs stormed out to a 21-7 lead and looked as good as the preseason hype suggested they'd be. With the game tied at 7 early in the second quarter, Georgia sophomore Fred Gibson fielded a kickoff and raced 91 yards for a touchdown and a 14-7 lead. It was the Bulldogs' first kickoff return for a touchdown since Andre Hastings returned one 89 yards against Kentucky in 1990.

Later in the second quarter, backup quarterback D.J. Shockley made his debut for the Bulldogs.

The *Parade Magazine* high school All-American was redshirted the previous season, and Georgia fans eagerly waited to see him play. His first college drive started at Clemson's 15-yard line, after Bulldogs safety Thomas Davis returned a shanked punt 18 yards. Shockley handed off to Smith on first down, and then Shockley ran for 6 yards. On third-and-4 at the Clemson 9, Shockley burst up the middle for a touchdown run and a 21-7 lead.

"It was definitely worth the wait," Shockley said. "Just coming in the game, the excitement of the crowd, I just kept saying, 'This was worth the wait.'"

The Tigers climbed back into the game with only eight seconds left in the first half when quarterback Willie Simmons threw a 21-yard touchdown pass to Kevin Youngblood, cutting Georgia's lead to 21-14 at halftime.

Then things got really scary for Georgia in the third quarter. With the Bulldogs seemingly driving for another touchdown, Smith dropped the pitch on a toss sweep. Clemson defensive end Bryant McNeal scooped the ball up and returned it 55 yards for a touchdown, tying the game at 21 with 9:54 left in the third.

	1st	2nd	3rd	4th	Final
CLEMSON	0	14	14	0	28
GEORGIA	7	14	0	10	31

SCORING SUMMARY

QTR	TEAM	PLAY		TIME
1st	GEORGIA	TD	Gary 4-yd. pass from Greene (Bennett kick)	0:51
2nd	CLEMSON	TD	Rambert 1-yd. run (Hunt kick)	11:23
2nd	GEORGIA	TD	Gibson 91-yd. kickoff return (Bennett kick)	10:54
2nd	GEORGIA	TD	Shockley 9-yd. run (Bennett kick)	8:10
2nd	CLEMSON	TD	Youngblood 21-yd. pass from Simmons (Hunt kick)	0:08
3rd	CLEMSON	TD	McNeal 55-yd. fumble recovery (Hunt kick)	9:54
3rd	CLEMSON	TD	Kelly 2-yd. run (Hunt kick)	2:25
4th	GEORGIA	TD	Edwards 24-yd. pass from Shockley (Bennett kick)	12:35
4th	GEORGIA	FG	Bennett 43-yd. field goal	5:19

OFFENSE

CLEMSON

PASSING	ATT	COMP	INT	YDS	TD
Simmons	37	17	1	165	1

RECEIVING	CATCHES	YDS	TD
Youngblood	6	66	1
McKelvey	2	24	0
Robinson	2	17	0
Rambert	2	12	0
Kelly	2	4	0
Elliott	1	20	0
Currie	1	12	0
Hall	1	10	0

RUSHING	RUSHES	YDS	TD
Rambert	10	35	1
Jasmin	5	30	0
Hamilton	3	18	0
Kelly	5	17	1
Simmons	8	-29	0

GEORGIA

PASSING	ATT	COMP	INT	YDS	TD
Greene	21	12	1	67	1
Shockley	4	3	0	50	1

RECEIVING	CATCHES	YDS	TD
Smith	4	16	0
Edwards	3	35	1
Gibson	3	28	0
Brown	2	21	0
Gary	2	13	1
Watson	1	4	0

RUSHING	RUSHES	YDS	TD
Smith	23	105	0
Shockley	5	10	1
Milton	2	5	0
Wall	1	0	0
Gibson	1	-6	0
Greene	4	-26	0

Boss Bailey sacked Willie Simmons for a 15-yard loss, forcing a fourth-quarter punt. The Bulldogs tied the game three plays later. Brant Sanderlin/AJC

On the ensuing kickoff, Gibson caught the ball at Georgia's 18, ran 3 yards and fumbled. The Tigers recovered at the Bulldogs' 21. Fortunately for the Bulldogs, Clemson kicker Aaron Hunt bounced a 37-yard field goal off the right upright. The game was still tied.

Georgia's offense went nowhere on its next possession, and the Tigers took over at their 24 with about seven minutes left in the third. The Tigers marched down the field, aided by two Georgia penalties, and Yusef Kelly scored on a 2-yard run, giving Clemson a 28-21 lead with 2:25 left in the third.

Early in the fourth quarter, Shockley had another short field to work after junior Damien Gary returned a punt 40 yards to the Clemson 31. On third-and-3, Shockley fired a 24-yard touchdown to senior Terrence Edwards, tying the game at 28 with about 12 1/2 minutes left. The Bulldogs went ahead 31-28 on kicker Billy Bennett's 43-yard field goal with 5:19 remaining

and then watched Hunt miss another field goal in the final two minutes.

"I was wondering what kind of heart and soul this team had," Richt said. "I am just proud of everybody. It was just a super job with the kicking game, and the defense bowed up when it needed to."

But Richt had some serious concerns about his offense and left the opener wondering what to do with his two quarterbacks. Greene, the reigning SEC freshman of the year, struggled mightily, completing only 12 of 21 passes for 67 yards with one touchdown and one interception. Shockley was 3-for-4 for 50 yards and a touchdown and ran for another score.

"I wanted D.J. to get his feet wet and get a feel for what college football is like," Richt said. "I think D.J. will play more. I like how he played. He didn't get flustered. I thought he was pretty accurate. I'm sure David wasn't thrilled about the whole game, but I still have a lot of confidence in him. He is still our starting quarterback, but D.J. will play more."

ABOVE:
Fred Gibson, trying to avoid Clemson's Travis Pugh, scored on a 91-yard kickoff return, the first Georgia kickoff return for a touchdown since Andre Hastings' in 1990. Brant Sanderlin/AJC

ABOVE:
Starter David Greene didn't have his best day, going 12-for-21 for 67 yards with a touchdown and an interception, but D.J. Shockley was there to back him up with two touchdowns. *Brant Sanderlin/AJC*

LEFT:
"I'm sure David wasn't thrilled about the whole game, but I still have a lot of confidence in him. He is still our starting quarterback," coach Mark Richt said of Greene. *Brant Sanderlin/AJC*

RIGHT:
Clemson kicker Aaron Hunt missed a field goal in the third quarter, but he also missed a 46-yarder with 1 minute, 43 seconds left that would have tied the game. *Brant Sanderlin/AJC*

SATURDAY, SEPTEMBER 14, 2002

GEORGIA 13, SOUTH CAROLINA 7

DOGS WEATHER STORM

Pollack's big plays help Georgia sink Gamecocks

COLUMBIA, S.C.—South Carolina quarterback Corey Jenkins didn't see what happened. Neither did Bulldogs defensive end David Pollack.

But a national TV audience and a soldout crowd in Williams-Brice Stadium watched what Pollack did. And, regardless of their allegiances, many fans still can't believe what they saw in Georgia's 13-7 victory.

With Georgia leading 3-0 in the fourth quarter, South Carolina snapped the ball from its 7-yard line. Pollack got around right tackle Watts Sanderson and leaped into the air to knock down Jenkins' pass. But the ball never got out of Jenkins' right hand, as Pollack stripped it and cradled it against his body.

"I was just trying to make a play, to get back there as fast as I could," Pollack said. "I wasn't looking at it. It just snuck into my hand. I just pulled it into my body. I don't know what I did. I have to look at that play on tape."

Said Jenkins: "I thought, 'Oh, well, incomplete pass.'"

But when Pollack fell to the turf in the end zone with the football still in his hands, an official raised his hands in the air, signaling a touchdown and a 10-0 lead for Georgia.

"Then I hear, 'Touchdown!'" Jenkins said. "I said, 'He caught it?' Then I said, 'Wow, is it going to be one of these nights again?'"

Even after Pollack's remarkable play, it looked like it was going to be another one of those nights for the Bulldogs. After losing to South Carolina in the final minutes the previous season, Georgia again watched the Gamecocks mount a furious rally.

After Pollack's touchdown, the Gamecocks came right back to close to 10-7. South Carolina scored just 1 minute, 35 seconds later when Jenkins hit senior Ryan Brewer for a 25-yard score after Brewer beat cornerback Bruce Thornton.

The Bulldogs increased their lead to 13-7 on junior Billy Bennett's 25-yard field goal with 2:54 left. Finally, the victory seemed secure.

But with less than two minutes remaining, Georgia's defense finally showed some cracks. Jenkins threw a 26-yard pass to Brewer on fourth-and-7 to the Bulldogs' 22. On the next play, Jenkins threw a screen pass to Andrew Pinnock, who ran for 11 yards to the Georgia 11. Jenkins then ran three straight times for a total of 9 yards, setting up a dramatic fourth-and-1 from the 2-yard line with only 20 seconds left.

After a timeout, the Gamecocks needed 1 yard for a first down or 2 yards for a touchdown. Jenkins lined up in the shotgun, took the snap, ran left and pitched to Pinnock. But Pollack rushed Jenkins on the pitch, and the ball hit Pinnock in the chest and was fumbled. Georgia safety Thomas Davis recovered to end the threat and seal the victory.

RIGHT:
Despite the bad weather that forced a 52-minute delay in the first half, Fred Gibson, catching the ball over South Carolina's Dunta Robinson, finished with six receptions for 116 yards.
Brant Sanderlin/AJC

ABOVE:

David Greene was 11-for-19 for 169 yards and no interceptions but failed to get the Bulldogs into the end zone.

Brant Sanderlin/AJC

"We were running the option," Pinnock said. "Their guy came off the edge quick. I should have been expecting the pitch to come fast. I dropped the pitch. We lost the game."

Georgia linebacker Boss Bailey said the Bulldogs were prepared for the option play. There were several Georgia players between Pinnock and the end zone on the left side of the field.

"The whole time, we were saying, 'Watch for the option, watch for the option,'" Bailey said. "It gives them a two-way threat. We were prepared for it, and we defended it perfectly. I think [Pinnock] looked up and saw that he had a lot of red hats right there at him.

I think that kind of frustrated him a little bit, and that's why the fumble happened."

Jenkins said he thought his teammate would have scored the game-winning touchdown if Pinnock had caught the pitch cleanly.

"He catches that ball cleanly and runs straight ahead; I don't see how anybody stops him," Jenkins said.

It was a strange ending to an even stranger game. The first half lasted two hours, 15 minutes because of a 52-minute lightning delay in the first quarter. There was only one scoring drive in the first 30 minutes, Bennett's 22-yard field goal on the opening possession.

	1st	2nd	3rd	4th	Final
GEORGIA	3	0	0	10	13
SOUTH CAROLINA	0	0	0	7	7

SCORING SUMMARY

QTR	TEAM	PLAY		TIME
1st	Georgia	FG	Bennett 22-yd. field goal	12:54
4th	Georgia	TD	Pollack 0-yd. interception return (Bennett kick)	13:58
4th	SC	TD	Brewer 25-yd. pass from Jenkins (Weaver kick)	12:23
4th	Georgia	FG	Bennett 25-yd. field goal	2:54

OFFENSE

GEORGIA

PASSING	ATT	COMP	INT	YDS	TD
Greene	19	11	0	169	0
Shockley	3	0	0	0	0

RECEIVING	CATCHES	YDS	TD
Gibson	6	116	0
Gary	2	7	0
Brown	1	20	0
Watson	1	16	0
Edwards	1	10	0

RUSHING	RUSHES	YDS	TD
Smith	27	103	0
Shockley	4	17	0
Wall	1	14	0
Browning	1	3	0
Greene	4	-7	0

SOUTH CAROLINA

PASSING	ATT	COMP	INT	YDS	TD
Jenkins	24	14	1	180	1
Pinkins	3	2	0	33	0

RECEIVING	CATCHES	YDS	TD
Brewer	7	106	1
Ages	4	56	0
Pinnock	2	25	0
Thomas	2	23	0
Gause	1	3	0

RUSHING	RUSHES	YDS	TD
Jenkins	17	101	0
Pinnock	11	27	0
Irons	4	24	0
Robinson	5	5	0
Pinkins	5	1	0

There were four turnovers, a missed field goal by the Gamecocks and appearances by four quarterbacks. South Carolina outgained the Bulldogs 371 yards to 297 yards, but the Gamecocks had four turnovers, including two lost fumbles at Georgia's 2-yard line.

The Bulldogs had chances to pull ahead after the weather delay. After South Carolina's Chavez Donnings fumbled a punt return at the Gamecocks' 12 in the first quarter, Bulldogs freshman Tyson Browning fumbled on the next play. Late in the second quarter, Georgia drove from its 3-yard line to the 39, but sophomore receiver Fred Gibson fumbled after a catch.

But South Carolina was never able to capitalize on Georgia's mistakes, either.

"This was really hard," South Carolina coach Lou Holtz said. "The kids are hurting right now. This was a heartbreaker."

But the Gamecocks' agony was Georgia's euphoria. The Bulldogs had never lost three games in a row to South Carolina, which handed Georgia heartbreaking losses in each of the two previous seasons. Now, the No. 9-ranked Bulldogs would take a 2-0 record into nonconference games against Division I-AA Northwestern State of Louisiana and New Mexico State.

The Bulldogs would have to play those games without backup quarterback D.J. Shockley, who broke his right foot while running off the field. For now, Georgia's two-quarterback system was on hold, and sophomore David Greene would lead the charge.

"There was just so much building up in the offseason for this game," Bailey said. "They had us two down, and we wanted this one so bad. We came in here, and we got it."

ABOVE:
Was it a fumble, an incomplete pass or an interception? No one knew at first except the official. But in a play that will be talked about for years to come, David Pollack intercepted Corey Jenkins in the end zone to give the Bulldogs a 10-0 lead. *Brant Sanderlin/AJC*

ABOVE:

*Tony Gilbert and the Bulldogs held Andrew Pinnock to 27
yards on 11 carries. Gilbert led the team with nine tackles.*

Brant Sanderlin/AJC

ABOVE:
*Tony Gilbert joins Georgia fans in the celebration after grabbing
a branch from the hedges at Williams-Brice Stadium.*
Brant Sanderlin/AJC

14

AGE: 20

DAVID GREENE

Rick Greene was sitting amid a sea of orange in Tennessee's Neyland Stadium on a Saturday afternoon last season, but he was as red as Georgia's football helmets.

Greene, the father of Bulldogs quarterback David Greene, was at his wits' end with the officials, and everyone sitting in his section was hearing about it.

"I can see he gets his calmness from his mother," said a Georgia fan sitting in front of him.

The truth is, Greene's mother, Kay, was right next to her husband screaming her lungs out.

"I was yelling my head off, but Rick was ready to blow a blood vessel," she said. "I get emotional. Our whole family is like that. I don't know where David gets his calmness from."

David Greene, a sophomore from Snellville, Ga., has been considerably more composed in his first two seasons with the Bulldogs. The first left-handed quarterback to start for Georgia since 1956, Greene has already led the Bulldogs to five fourth-quarter comebacks, including two of the more memorable ones in school history.

At Tennessee last season, Greene directed a five-play, 59-yard scoring drive in 39 seconds and threw the game-winning touchdown to fullback Verron Haynes with five seconds left. It was the Bulldogs' first victory at Knoxville in 21 years.

At Auburn this season, Greene threw the game-winning touchdown to junior Michael Johnson on fourth-and-15 with 85 seconds left. That victory put the Bulldogs in their first SEC championship game, where they beat Arkansas 30-3 to win their first conference title since 1982.

Brant Sanderlin/AJC

HOMETOWN:
SNELLVILLE, GA.

CLASS: SOPHOMORE

QUARTERBACK

"His birth certificate might say he's [20] years old, but he plays quarterback like he's a junior or senior," said Bulldogs offensive tackle Jon Stinchcomb.

Greene wasn't always this composed. He said he vomited before every game during his junior season at South Gwinnett High School in 1998.

"I used to get nervous in my junior year of high school," Greene said. "I told myself, 'You've got to stay calm if you're going to play to your potential.' Now, I don't really have a problem with staying calm. Every time I'm on the field, I'm comfortable with it."

And it certainly showed on the field this season. In his second season as a starter, Greene led the SEC in passing efficiency and was named to the Associated Press' All-SEC first team, over more highly regarded quarterbacks Casey Clausen of Tennessee, Rex Grossman of Florida and Eli Manning of Ole Miss. Greene also was named MVP of the SEC championship game.

Georgia coach Mark Richt, in his second season at Georgia, spent more than a decade coaching quarterbacks at Florida State. He helped produce two Heisman Trophy-winning quarterbacks for the Seminoles — Charlie Ward in 1993 and Chris Weinke in 2000. Four other FSU quarterbacks went on to play in the NFL during Richt's tenure there. But only Weinke, Richt says, had a better grasp of his offense than Greene this early in his career.

"And Weinke was a grown man, too," Richt said. "He was [25] years old by then."

Greene showed maturity beyond his years on and off the field this season. He threw 22 touchdowns and only eight interceptions in the first 13 games. Going into the Jan. 1 Sugar Bowl against Florida State, he needed two touchdown passes to tie Eric Zeier's single-season school record.

"He's an accurate passer, and he's very calm, and not a lot bothers him," Richt said. "What we're doing is not rocket science, and a lot of it is fairly simple concepts. But if you're giving him 100 examples, that's pretty difficult."

Richt has so much trust in Greene that he allows him to make audibles at the line of scrimmage on nearly any play. While other quarterbacks tend to look to the sideline for plays to check into, Richt says Greene does it on his own. On most plays, Greene can check into one of two running plays or a pass. He audibles out of the protection scheme and gives his receivers as many as four or five different pass routes.

Most of the time, Richt said, "He is calling what we would call."

Georgia defensive end David Pollack, who played with Greene in a youth football league in suburban Atlanta, said he isn't surprised by his friend's success. Even when they were 8 years old, Pollack said, he knew Greene was different.

"The coach would signal in a number, and he would look at the number on his wristband to see which play to call," Pollack said. "He was 8 years old. Who does that stuff when you're 8?"

GEORGIA 45, NORTHWESTERN STATE 7

MONEY WELL SPENT

Bulldogs beat up on Division I-AA Northwestern State

ATHENS, Ga. — Amount of money Georgia wants from Tulane for backing out of its contract to play football this season in Athens? $1 million. Cost of bringing in Division I-AA Northwestern State to replace the Green Wave? $400,000. A get-well win for Georgia's offense? Priceless.

After less-than-spectacular performances by the Bulldogs in their first two games, Georgia's offense shredded the Demons in a 45-7 rout at Sanford Stadium.

The result was predictable against an opponent that was added to the schedule six months before, played in front of 3,500 fans at Delaware State the previous week and traveled 11 hours by bus to Athens. But the Bulldogs gladly took the victory nonetheless.

"I think this game was just what we needed to get our confidence back," Bulldogs receiver Damien Gary said. "Those guys didn't come in here to roll over."

But Northwestern State didn't exactly fire out of the gates, either.

BELOW:
David Greene seldom had to scramble on his way to a 26-for-43 day in which he threw for four touchdowns and 346 yards.
Brant Sanderlin/AJC

Georgia quarterback David Greene threw a 42-yard pass to sophomore Fred Gibson on the first play from scrimmage. Two plays later, Greene completed another pass to Gibson, who lost a fumble inside the Demons' 15-yard line.

The Bulldogs got the ball back at Northwestern State's 44-yard line, and Greene threw a 5-yard touchdown pass to sophomore Reggie Brown with 11:47 left in the first quarter, giving Georgia a 7-0 lead.

On the Demons' ensuing possession, Georgia safety Sean Jones blocked Chris Stegall's punt. Cornerback Bruce Thornton scooped up the ball and returned it 12 yards for a touchdown and a 14-0 lead. It was the Bulldogs' first touchdown off a blocked punt since Glenn Ford did it against Vanderbilt in 1997.

"That doesn't happen all that often," Thornton said. "I tried to pick it up, then I kicked it. Then I saw one of my teammates and I tipped it forward. I wanted to score that touchdown. It reminded me of my running back days."

ABOVE:
"I think this game was just what we needed to get our confidence back," said Damien Gary, who had three catches for 43 yards, including this one against Kerry Goldsmith. Brant Sanderlin/AJC

Said Jones: "I got the blocked punt, so I guess I let him get the touchdown. I just tried to put my head down and run upfield. The next thing I knew, I was at the punter. I knew I would be able to get to it."

Georgia's next two drives left coach Mark Richt baffled. After driving into position for another touchdown, Greene threw a ball into the left flat that was intercepted by Demons cornerback Jerry Goldsmith. Greene was sacked for a 10-yard loss on the first play of the Bulldogs' next series, and Georgia was forced to punt.

"We were a little shoddy early," Richt said.

But Georgia's defense stood firm, and the Bulldogs went ahead 21-0 on Greene's 5-yard touchdown pass to fullback J.T. Wall. It looked like Georgia would go

ahead 28-0 after Gary's 80-yard punt return for a touchdown early in the second quarter, but the score was nullified by a holding penalty.

Instead, Georgia took the ball at its 30-yard line and marched 40 yards in 10 plays. The Bulldogs settled for Billy Bennett's 47-yard field goal, which gave them a 24-0 lead with 7:50 left in the first half. Georgia made it 31-0 when Greene threw a 12-yard touchdown to senior Terrence Edwards with 17 seconds left in the half.

Gary admitted the Bulldogs might have been taking the Demons a little lightly to start the game.

"It's hard," he said. "You have to get yourself pumped up for a game. You kind of expect it's not going to be like you're playing Tennessee. You have to get

	1st	2nd	3rd	4th	Final
NORTHWESTERN STATE	0	0	7	0	7
GEORGIA	14	17	7	7	45

SCORING SUMMARY

QTR	TEAM	PLAY		TIME
1st	**Georgia**	TD	Brown 5-yd. pass from Greene (Bennett kick)	11:47
1st	**Georgia**	TD	Thornton 12-yd. blocked punt return (Bennett kick)	10:10
2nd	**Georgia**	TD	Wall 5-yd. pass from Greene (Bennett kick)	13:49
2nd	**Georgia**	FG	Bennett 47-yd. field goal	7:50
2nd	**Georgia**	TD	Edwards 12-yd. pass from Greene (Bennett kick)	0:17
3rd	**NSU**	TD	Harrison 11-yd. pass from Magee (Hebert kick)	10:24
3rd	**Georgia**	TD	Edwards 3-yd. pass from Greene (Bennett kick)	6:55
4th	**Georgia**	TD	Johnson 11-yd. pass from Phillips (Bennett kick)	5:54

OFFENSE

NORTHWESTERN STATE

PASSING	ATT	COMP	INT	YDS	TD
Magee	23	17	1	150	1
Beach	11	4	1	61	0

RECEIVING	CATCHES	YDS	TD
Harrison	10	81	1
Zeigler	3	42	0
Bell	1	34	0
Sampson	1	19	0
Gatlin	1	13	0
May	1	9	0
West	1	6	0
Smith	1	6	0
Johnese	1	3	0
Clark	1	-2	0

RUSHING	RUSHES	YDS	TD
Sampson	13	36	0
Lofton	7	18	0
Bell	2	7	0
Sanders	2	5	0
Johnese	6	3	0
Harrison	1	2	0
May	2	1	0
Magee	3	-4	0
Beach	2	-11	0

GEORGIA

PASSING	ATT	COMP	INT	YDS	TD
Greene	43	26	1	346	4
Phillips	4	3	0	48	1

RECEIVING	CATCHES	YDS	TD
Gibson	8	134	0
Edwards	6	76	2
Johnson	3	44	1
Gary	3	43	0
Brown	3	33	1
Smith	2	39	0
Watson	2	17	0
Wall	1	5	1
Milton	1	3	0

RUSHING	RUSHES	YDS	TD
Smith	8	70	0
Browning	6	53	0
Milton	4	24	0
Greene	6	3	0
Wall	1	1	0
Snyder	1	1	0
Powell	1	-4	0
Phillips	1	-6	0

Shelton Sampson led Northwestern State with 36 yards rushing, but Robert Geathers and the defense kept the Demons' running game in check, holding them to 55 yards. Brant Sanderlin/AJC

yourself jacked up. If you don't, the other team might come out and surprise you and score some points, and maybe then it's too late to get jacked up. It's hard to get emotionally prepared."

Richt said his team had no reason to be overconfident after its performance in its first two games, narrow wins over Clemson and South Carolina.

"We had so much to prove," Richt said. "A lot of times if a team is on a roll, you have to worry about being complacent. I was more concerned about our confidence."

Northwestern State's only touchdown came early in the third quarter, with quarterback Kevin Magee throwing an 11-yard touchdown to Freddie Harrison.

Georgia added two more touchdowns in the second half, with Greene throwing a 3-yard scoring pass to Edwards. Richt called off the Dogs after that and sent in his second team. Third-string quarterback Cory Phillips threw an 11-yard touchdown to junior Michael Johnson with six minutes left in the game.

After sputtering in its first two games, Georgia's offense seemed to perform better with one quarterback rather than two. Greene tied a school record with four touchdown passes and threw for 346 yards on 26-for-43 passing. Gibson set a school record with his seventh 100-yard receiving game, finishing with eight catches for 134 yards. Tailback Musa Smith ran for 70 yards on eight touches.

"We won those first two games with an eight-cylinder engine that has only two cylinders hitting offensively," Richt said. "We're fortunate to be winning. I was pleased we got better."

ABOVE:
Just like the rest of the Northwestern State defense, Jerry Goldsmith had trouble keeping up with Fred Gibson, who had 126 of his 134 receiving yards in the first half. Brant Sanderlin/AJC

ABOVE:
The Georgia defense allowed 266 total yards but held Northwestern State to seven points. Brant Sanderlin/AJC

Georgia was playing its first game without backup quarterback D.J. Shockley, who broke his foot at South Carolina. Richt said Shockley's absence probably had little to do with Greene's improvement.

"[Greene] started out not as hot as last year," Richt said. "But we played different opening opponents than we did last year. They were two quality football teams on both sides, and the South Carolina game wasn't exactly played in ideal conditions. All those things together will have an effect on how much offense you'll have in a game."

Georgia's defense continued to play surprisingly well. The Bulldogs intercepted two passes, recovered a fumble and held the Demons to 55 rushing yards (1.4 per carry).

"One-double-A, one-A, it really doesn't matter who we were playing," senior tackle Jon Stinchcomb said. "We just needed to have a positive game. For the first two games, we won, but we came back on Monday and scratched our heads. For the offense to have a productive day like this, hopefully it will serve as a catalyst."

ABOVE:
Freshman DeMario Minter (2) and teammates try to stay cool on the bench during the Bulldogs' victory.
Brant Sanderlin/AJC

FOLLOWING PAGE:
The serious faces of the Georgia marching band belie the ease with which the Bulldogs handled Northwestern State, winning 45-7.
Brant Sanderlin/AJC

GEORGIA 41, NEW MEXICO STATE 10

DOGS DO "JUST ENOUGH" TO CORRAL AGGIES

Gary's punt return for touchdown sparks Bulldogs from early deficit

ATHENS, Ga. — As Georgia coach Mark Richt wandered through his team's locker room after the 41-10 win over New Mexico State, quarterback David Greene stopped Richt before he walked out the door.

"Was it frustrating to watch?" Greene asked his coach.

Richt told his quarterback no, but that wasn't what Georgia's second-year coach told reporters after watching his offense sputter for the third time in four games.

While No. 8-ranked Georgia improved to 4-0 for the fourth time in six seasons, dropped balls and misfired passes were again a big cause of concern. In the second half, the Aggies more than doubled the Bulldogs' offensive production in plays (47 to 21) and yards (149 to 74).

"We're good, but we want to be great," Richt said. "Our offense was pretty poor in the second half. We didn't move the ball well. It was just very, very frustrating with what happened. Those guys are going to look at the film and see what could have been. What could have been was an awful lot of yards and an awful lot of points."

But Georgia fans weren't as concerned about what could have been as much as what would be. Starting with the game at Alabama, the stakes would get much higher. If the Bulldogs were going to compete for their first SEC championship since 1982, the offense would

have to start hitting on all cylinders. The Bulldogs gained only 299 yards against New Mexico State, the third time during the season the Bulldogs had failed to total at least 300.

"Right now, I think we're playing just well enough to win," Greene said. "I don't think we've come close to our potential yet."

Against the Aggies, Greene misfired on three long passes to Terrence Edwards and Fred Gibson that would have been easy touchdowns. Greene also threw an interception on the Bulldogs' first play, allowing the Aggies to take a 7-0 lead in front of a stunned crowd of 86,520 in Sanford Stadium.

But the game turned late in the first quarter. After Georgia's defense held the Aggies to three plays and a punt inside New Mexico State's 20-yard line, punter Brian Copple boomed a 47-yard punt to Bulldogs receiver Damien Gary. Gary was able to run under the angled punt, catch it at the Georgia 29-yard line and spin, dodging the initial tackler. Three more Aggies missed Gary as he raced down the right sideline, before tight end Ben Watson eliminated the fifth would-be tackler with a downfield block. Gary's 71-yard punt return for a touchdown tied the game at 7 with 2:50 left in the first quarter.

RIGHT:
"Right now, I think we're playing just well enough to win," David Greene said after throwing for two touchdowns and an interception. Brant Sanderlin/AJC

ABOVE:

The Aggies scored on an early touchdown and a late-game field goal, but that was all they would get against the tough Bulldogs defense. Brant Sanderlin/AJC

"I doubt anybody's getting popcorn during punts anymore," Richt said. "It seems like we either block one or score on the return."

Gary scored again on Georgia's next possession, catching a 20-yard pass from Greene for a 14-7 lead. Gary made five catches for 36 yards and returned four punts for 94 yards and a touchdown. Gary didn't get many more opportunities on punt returns after his touchdown. The Aggies purposely punted the ball out of bounds, with one punt traveling 18 yards before hitting the sideline. In all, five of New Mexico State's punts went out of bounds and one was blocked.

"He's the best I've ever seen on punt returns," Greene said. "We don't worry about Damien too much. If he doesn't fair catch, he always seems to make the first guy miss and usually the second or third. I've been here three years, and I don't think I've ever seen the first one bring him down."

Gary's touchdown return sparked the Bulldogs, who scored 27 points in the second quarter, the most points scored in a quarter since they scored 28 in the first quarter of a 70-6 rout of Northeast Louisiana in 1994.

Greene recovered to throw two touchdowns, and sophomore tailback Musa Smith ran for two more scores, giving the Bulldogs a 34-7 lead at halftime. But Georgia's offense never found the end zone in the second half and got to the Aggies' side of the field only once.

"We're very close to being unstoppable," Gary said. "There might be an overthrown pass here, a dropped ball there, or a missed blitz pickup. We're just so close to being a great offense. But we're on the brink of breaking it."

Richt had reasons for optimism. Georgia's defense, which lost seven starters from the previous year, allowed only one touchdown for the third game in a row. The

	1st	2nd	3rd	4th	Final
NEW MEXICO STATE	7	0	0	3	10
GEORGIA	7	27	0	7	41

SCORING SUMMARY

QTR	TEAM	PLAY		TIME
1st	NMS	TD	Dombrowksi 2-yd. run (Aguiniga kick)	10:51
1st	Georgia	TD	Gary 71-yd. punt return (Bennett kick)	2:50
2nd	Georgia	TD	Gary 20-yd. pass from Greene (Bennett kick)	14:55
2nd	Georgia	TD	Smith 10-yd. run (Bennett kick)	9:48
2nd	Georgia	TD	Edwards 10-yd. pass from Greene (PAT fails)	6:27
2nd	Georgia	TD	Smith 13-yd. run (Bennett kick)	3:21
4th	Georgia	TD	Curry 78-yd. interception return (Bennett kick)	12:02
4th	NMS	FG	Aguiniga 32-yd. field goal	1:32

—— OFFENSE ——

NEW MEXICO STATE

PASSING	ATT	COMP	INT	YDS	TD
Dombrowski	26	11	1	152	0
Brady	5	3	0	27	0
Pierce	3	3	0	8	0
Scaffidi	2	1	0	7	0

RECEIVING	CATCHES	YDS	TD
Briscoe	5	97	0
Winston	3	35	0
Higgins	3	8	0
Lumpkin	2	15	0
Duncan	1	13	0
Williams	1	10	0
Jenkins	1	7	0
Mouton	1	5	0
Bostic	1	4	0

RUSHING	RUSHES	YDS	TD
Mouton	7	26	0
Taylor	7	19	0
Bostic	5	16	0
Dixon	2	16	0
Higgins	7	8	0
Dombrowski	13	3	1
Okamura	1	2	0
Scaffidi	1	1	0
Winston	2	-1	0
Pierce	3	-9	0

GEORGIA

PASSING	ATT	COMP	INT	YDS	TD
Greene	34	19	1	207	2
Phillips	2	0	0	0	0

RECEIVING	CATCHES	YDS	TD
Edwards	5	55	1
Gary	5	36	1
Watson	3	53	0
Smith	2	14	0
Gibson	2	11	0
McClendon	1	21	0
Brown	1	17	0

RUSHING	RUSHES	YDS	TD
Smith	12	79	2
Milton	3	14	0
Browning	1	1	0
Greene	3	-1	0

Damien Gary's 71-yard punt return for a touchdown led coach Mark Richt to say: "I doubt anybody's getting popcorn during punts anymore." Brant Sanderlin/AJC

Bulldogs' special teams and defense had scored five touchdowns in the first four games.

Along with Gary's punt return for a touchdown, junior safety Kentrell Curry returned an interception 78 yards for another score. The Bulldogs recorded six sacks, and the Aggies averaged less than 2 yards on 48 rushes. Defensive end David Pollack had three sacks, and junior Shedrick Wynn, who missed the first three games because of a suspension, had two more.

"We're within striking distance of being pretty good," Richt said. "Anytime your defense and kicking teams play well, you've got a chance to win every game you play. If our offense gets over the hump, and I think they're a lot closer to getting over the hump than they were two weeks ago, we've got a chance. We've just got to put it all together."

It had to happen sooner than later for the Bulldogs. They had never won in seven games against Alabama in Tuscaloosa, and No. 11-ranked Tennessee would try to break a two-game losing streak to Georgia when it visited Athens on Oct. 12.

"We have to take it to another level," Watson said. "Every game is a must-win, but we've got to beat Alabama and Tennessee if we're going to compete for a championship."

WE'RE VERY CLOSE TO BEING UNSTOPPABLE.

— BULLDOGS RECEIVER DAMIEN GARY

ABOVE:
Misfires and dropped passes, including this one by Fred Gibson, frustrated the Bulldogs. Gibson finished with two catches for 11 yards. Brant Sanderlin/AJC

WE'RE WITHIN STRIKING DISTANCE OF BEING PRETTY GOOD. ANYTIME YOUR DEFENSE AND KICKING TEAMS PLAY WELL, YOU'VE GOT A CHANCE TO WIN EVERY GAME YOU PLAY.

— BULLDOGS COACH MARK RICHT

ABOVE:
Junior Shedrick Wynn, lifting up Chris Clemons, made two sacks in his season debut, which was delayed three games because of a suspension. *Brant Sanderlin/AJC*

RIGHT:
David Pollack forces Paul Dombrowski to fumble during one of his three sacks. The Bulldogs finished with six sacks.
Brant Sanderlin/AJC

HOMETOWN: TENNILLE, GA.

CLASS: SENIOR

TERRENCE EDWARDS

I n his four seasons at Georgia, receiver Terrence Edwards has learned how fickle college football fans can be.

Despite leaving Georgia as the school's all-time leader in receptions, receiving yards and touchdown catches, Edwards has been vilified for dropping too many passes in critical situations.

The condemnation reached a fever pitch this season, after Edwards dropped a long pass in the final minutes of Georgia's 20-13 loss to Florida in Jacksonville. If Edwards had caught the pass, with two and a half minutes left, he might have scored the game-tying touchdown. Instead, what might have been the defining moment of his career slipped away.

With the clock winding down in Alltel Stadium, Edwards broke into the clear after Florida safety Guss Scott slipped on the turf. Quarterback David Greene lofted a pass to Edwards, who jumped to catch it. But the ball bounced off his hands about the Gators' 30-yard line.

"I knew I was open, but I didn't know where the defender was," Edwards said. "I just tried to get to the ball at the highest point so [Scott] couldn't get it. I just closed my hands and it bounced off. I would have tried to catch the ball a different way if I'd known he'd fallen down. I would have caught it over the shoulder, instead of attacking it.

"I made a mistake," he said. "I'm human."

After the Bulldogs' only loss of the regular season, Edwards was criticized on radio talk shows

Brant Sanderlin/AJC

AGE: 23

RECEIVER

and on Internet message boards. One fan left a sarcastic message on his answering machine at home. Edwards' parents ripped Georgia fans, saying they couldn't wait for their son to graduate. But Edwards said he got more support from other fans.

"More people are with me than against me," Edwards said. "But I guess there's some people who've never made a mistake."

One group of Georgia fans really wanted to show their support for Edwards. They leased a billboard-sized thank-you note that conveyed this message to him: "Thanks Terrence For 4 Great Years . . . The No. 1 WR in UGA History — The Fans."

The billboard was posted near Edwards' hometown of Tennille, between Macon and Augusta in middle Georgia. Ted Kohn of Tybee Island, Ga., read the negative comments from Edwards' parents and wanted to show his support. He got the idea for a billboard while driving through Tennille on his way to Athens for a game.

"I thought his mom and dad could see it every time they went to the bank, Wal-Mart, the post office or wherever," Kohn said.

Kohn said it cost $650 to lease the billboard for 30 days. He raised the money by posting a message on the Dawgvent, a popular Internet message board. Edwards said he appreciated their support.

"I think the bad has brought out all the good," Edwards said. "A couple of people have been negative, but most have been really appreciative."

Edwards bounced back from the drop in the Florida game, catching five passes for 90 yards and a touchdown in the Bulldogs' 31-17 victory over Ole Miss. He separated his shoulder late in that game and didn't play in the 24-21 victory over Auburn the next week. Edwards returned for the SEC championship game, catching seven passes for 92 yards in the 30-3 victory over Arkansas. He became the SEC's all-time leader in receiving yards in that game.

Edwards was a quarterback in high school, but his career at receiver started fast during his freshman season in 1999. He had 10 catches for 196 yards and two touchdowns in his first game against Utah State. Edwards became the first freshman since Lindsay Scott in 1978 to lead the Bulldogs in receiving and tied the school record with nine touchdown catches. He had nearly identical production as a sophomore, but then his numbers slipped as a junior in 2001.

In his first season in new coach Mark Richt's offense, Edwards was benched midway through the 2001 season for dropping too many passes. He didn't catch a pass in last year's 24-10 loss to the Gators, the only time during his career that he didn't catch a ball in a game.

But Edwards worked harder in the offseason and vowed to come back stronger. He finished the season with 1,044 yards, a Georgia record, and finished his career with 30 touchdowns and 204 receptions, both second in the SEC.

"After we made him second team last year, instead of getting bitter about it or getting negative, he did what he had to do to get his job back," Richt said. "He worked hard in the offseason and was our most consistent receiver in preseason camp. I'm glad to see how he responded."

SATURDAY, OCTOBER 5, 2002

GEORGIA 27, ALABAMA 25

MAN ENOUGH

Bulldogs answer Dye's challenge to get first victory in Tuscaloosa

TUSCALOOSA, Ala.—Are you man enough? That was the question former Auburn coach Pat Dye challenged his alma mater with, and the No. 7-ranked Bulldogs flexed their collective muscles in an impressive 27-25 win at Alabama. It was Georgia's first victory in Tuscaloosa.

The Bulldogs moved to 5-0 for the first time since 1982, the last season they won the SEC championship. And coupled with Florida's loss at Ole Miss, Georgia sat alone atop the SEC East for the first time since the conference split into two divisions in 1992.

"It's just a great victory," Georgia coach Mark Richt said. "I'm proud to be with a group of men that made some history here."

Few really believed Georgia could run the ball or stop the run against Alabama. The Bulldogs' loudest critic was Dye, an All-SEC lineman at Georgia in the late 1950s and early 1960s. On a radio show in Birmingham the week before, Dye said Alabama would "whip" Georgia because the

BELOW:

Terrence Edwards beat Anthony Madison early in the fourth quarter for a 37-yard reception that gave Georgia a 24-12 lead.
Brant Sanderlin/AJC

Bulldogs weren't "man enough" to beat the Crimson Tide.

"I'm glad Pat Dye made that statement," Georgia running back Musa Smith said. "I took it personally. He really triggered something in our hearts, and I think it's going to carry the rest of the season."

It carried Georgia against Alabama, which entered the game leading the SEC in rush defense. But the Bulldogs outrushed Alabama 161-109, and Smith ran for 126 yards on 21 carries. Alabama had averaged 318 yards on the ground in its previous three games.

"What [Dye] said helped motivate us some," Richt said. "It does help a little bit when you're tired and want to quit and your manhood's questioned."

In the end, though, it was Georgia's smallest player who showed just how tough the Bulldogs were. With Alabama leading 25-24, junior kicker Billy Bennett made a 32-yard field goal with 38 seconds left, helping the Bulldogs rally after they blew a 12-point lead in the fourth

ABOVE:
Terrence Edwards, stiff-arming Charles Jones, finished with 73 yards on five catches and had 52 return yards. Brant Sanderlin/AJC

quarter. It was Bennett's second game-winning field goal of the season.

Georgia safety Thomas Davis intercepted Alabama quarterback Brodie Croyle's pass on the next play from scrimmage to seal the victory.

"I was just thinking that we do this in practice every day," Bennett said. "I saw time running down and I thought, 'Oh goodness, this is coming down to me.' You always dream of making a kick like that with the game on the line. This is sweet."

It came down to Bennett because of Georgia's defense and special teams. After Bulldogs defensive end David Pollack sacked Croyle, junior Damien Gary's 15-yard punt return gave Georgia the ball back at the Alabama 34 with 3:45 to play. And if there were any questions about the Bulldogs' manhood, they were answered on their game-winning drive.

The Bulldogs ran right at the Crimson Tide's vaunted defense, as Smith gained 19 yards on five straight carries. David Greene ran a quarterback sneak to the middle of the field to position Bennett's field-goal attempt.

"At that point we just wanted to milk the clock and make them use all their timeouts," Richt said. "I

just wanted to make one first down and then give Billy a chance to kick it."

Said Smith: "What people don't understand about this team is that we're going to do whatever we have to do to win the game."

It seemed like the Bulldogs were going to do everything to lose it earlier in the fourth quarter. Trailing 24-12, Alabama got back into the game when Croyle faked a handoff to tailback Shaud Williams, then leaped over cornerback Bruce Thornton across the goal line to cut it to 24-19 with 9:27 left.

On Georgia's ensuing possession, Greene threw to the left side for sophomore receiver Fred Gibson, who bobbled the pass. Alabama cornerback Charlie Peprah stole the ball out of Gibson's hands and raced 35 yards for the Crimson Tide's second touchdown in 63 seconds.

"I stole it and just went to the house," Peprah said. "I just thought, 'We need to put them away.'"

After Peprah's touchdown, Croyle tried to score a two-point conversion on a run to the right side but was stopped short of the goal line. Alabama was supposed to run an option right, but Georgia cut off Croyle, forcing him to cut back inside. Croyle lunged

	1st	2nd	3rd	4th	Final
GEORGIA	7	7	3	10	27
ALABAMA	3	6	3	13	25

SCORING SUMMARY

QTR	TEAM	PLAY		TIME
1st	Georgia	TD	Smith 15-yd. run (Bennett kick)	9:04
1st	Alabama	FG	Ziifle 47-yd. field goal	5:16
2nd	Georgia	TD	Gibson 42-yd. pass from Greene (Bennett kick)	8:15
2nd	Alabama	TD	Fulgham 30-yd. pass from Croyle (PAT fails)	0:51
3rd	Georgia	FG	Bennett 43-yd. field goal	10:14
3rd	Alabama	FG	Bostick 36-yd. field goal	0:18
4th	Georgia	TD	Edwards 37-yd. pass from Greene (Bennett kick)	13:32
4th	Alabama	TD	Croyle 1-yd. run (Bostick kick)	9:27
4th	Alabama	TD	Peprah 35-yd. interception return (2-pt. conv. fails)	8:24
4th	Georgia	FG	Bennett 32-yd. field goal	0:38

OFFENSE

GEORGIA

PASSING	ATT	COMP	INT	YDS	TD
Greene	27	15	2	224	2

RECEIVING	CATCHES	YDS	TD
Edwards	5	73	1
Gibson	4	85	1
Gary	4	46	0
Johnson	1	12	0
Brown	1	8	0

RUSHING	RUSHES	YDS	TD
Smith	21	126	1
Milton	6	28	0
Wall	4	25	0
Browning	1	-1	0
Greene	9	-15	0

ALABAMA

PASSING	ATT	COMP	INT	YDS	TD
Croyle	29	16	1	197	1

RECEIVING	CATCHES	YDS	TD
Williams	6	44	0
Fulgham	3	63	1
Johnston	3	33	0
Collins	2	20	0
Fletcher	1	24	0
Clarke	1	13	0

RUSHING	RUSHES	YDS	TD
Hudson	3	45	0
Williams	10	44	0
Beard	15	23	0
Croyle	9	-3	1

David Pollack, Darrius Swain (98), Chris Clemons and the defense limited Alabama's leading rusher, Shaud Williams, to 44 yards on 10 carries. Brant Sanderlin/AJC

again for the goal line, "but the official said I didn't make it. I had to have been pretty close."

The Bulldogs couldn't pick up a first down on their next possession, but then the Georgia defense stuffed Alabama to set up the dramatic field-goal drive at the end.

Surprisingly, the Bulldogs opened the game by running right at the Crimson Tide. Smith gained 10 yards on his first two carries and then burst 17 yards for a first down to the Alabama 41. After a penalty gave Georgia a first down at the Tide 15, Smith scored on a toss sweep to the left side on the next play, giving the Bulldogs a 7-0 lead.

"The toss sweep was a bigger play for us than it has been for a long time," Richt said. "When they lined up to stop the run, I thought they were a little bit vulnerable to the toss."

Greene was picked off twice but still threw touchdowns to senior Terrence Edwards and Gibson, helping the Bulldogs go ahead 24-12 early in the fourth quarter. Greene finished 15-for-27 for 224 yards.

"Georgia football has been around a long time, so to do something like this is pretty sweet," Greene said. "A lot of people have doubted this team, but we never did."

As big as the Alabama win was, Georgia knew it had an even more manly test the next week against No. 10 Tennessee in Sanford Stadium. Georgia had not defeated a top-10 SEC team in Athens since 1976, when the No. 6-ranked Bulldogs beat No. 10 Alabama 21-0. Georgia had lost 13 of its previous 14 home games against ranked opponents; the one win came against No. 21 Tennessee in 2000.

"We did something important today," Richt said. "Now, we'll find out if we can build on it."

ABOVE:
Tailback Tony Milton had 28 yards on six carries.
Brant Sanderlin/AJC

IT'S JUST A GREAT VICTORY. I'M PROUD TO BE WITH A GROUP OF MEN THAT MADE SOME HISTORY HERE.

— BULLDOGS COACH MARK RICHT

ABOVE:
Coach Mark Richt and receiver Michael Johnson share the Bulldogs' first victory in Tuscaloosa after Billy Bennett's 32-yard field goal with 38 seconds left. Brant Sanderlin/AJC

ABOVE:
"Georgia football has been around a long time, so to do something like this is pretty sweet," said quarterback David Greene, who threw for two touchdowns. *Brant Sanderlin/AJC*

Quarterback Brodie Croyle appears to come up short, but officials ruled he had scored a touchdown for Alabama in the waning minutes of Georgia first-ever victory in Tuscaloosa. *Brant Sanderlin/AJC*

SATURDAY, OCTOBER 12, 2002

GEORGIA 18, TENNESSEE 13

TOP DOGS IN SEC EAST

Volunteers put up a fight but get knocked out

ATHENS — Six down, six to go. Or maybe more.

Georgia's football team reached the midpoint of its regular season undefeated with an 18-13 victory over Tennessee before 86,520 in Sanford Stadium.

Now, the Bulldogs were starting to dream about how successfully their season might end.

"This team has as much fighting heart as any I've ever been around," said Georgia coach Mark Richt, who served on the staff of two national championship teams at Florida State. "If we can improve, especially on offense, we can do something special."

The Bulldogs were 6-0 for the first time since 1982, and Georgia fans left Sanford Stadium with visions of their team's first Southeastern Conference championship in 20 years. Sweeping their remaining schedule would guarantee the Dogs a spot in the SEC championship game Dec. 7 at the Georgia Dome.

And after that? The national championship would be decided at the Fiesta Bowl on Jan. 3 in Tempe, Ariz.

"We've set lofty goals," said Georgia senior lineman Jon Stinchcomb. "To win championships. We're not bashful about our goals. We will not sell ourselves short of the apex of college football."

The Volunteers, ranked No. 10 but playing without starting quarterback Casey Clausen, were one of Georgia's biggest remaining hurdles in its quest for an SEC championship. From 1997 to 1999, the Bulldogs entered their game against Tennessee with a 4-0 record. The Vols beat them every time. But Georgia finally ended a nine-game losing streak to Tennessee in

2000, and with this victory, the Bulldogs had won three games in a row in the heated rivalry.

"What's so great about this team is that they really scrape and fight to win," said Georgia athletics director Vince Dooley, who coached the Bulldogs to their last SEC championship. "That's what you need to be a champion — a lot of heart. This team has it. There are no easy games, but I like what I see. They have developed an attitude, a feeling that they will win the game. That's important. And that's good."

The Bulldogs certainly looked like they were playing with confidence against the Volunteers. After Tennessee safety Rashad Baker intercepted a pass off receiver Terrence Edwards' hands on Georgia's second possession, the Bulldogs forced the Volunteers to punt from their 25-yard line.

Sophomore receiver Reggie Brown blocked Dustin Colquitt's punt, and the ball was deflected toward the end zone. Georgia tight end Ben Watson tried to pick it up near the goal line, but the ball rolled out of bounds in the end zone for a safety. The Bulldogs' third blocked punt of the season gave them a 2-0 lead with 3:50 left in the first quarter.

With Clausen sidelined with a hairline fracture in his collarbone, the Volunteers' offense struggled. Junior C.J. Leak started the game at quarterback but was pulled after two possessions for ineffectiveness and replaced by freshman James Banks.

Banks helped the Volunteers put together a lengthy drive early in the second quarter. After tailback Jabari Davis' 10-yard run gave the Vols a first down at Georgia's 35-yard line, the Bulldogs stuffed Tennessee on three

ABOVE:
Terrence Edwards, grabbing a pass in front of Tennessee's Willie Miles, led the Bulldogs with 115 yards receiving.

Brant Sanderlin/AJC

ABOVE:
A capacity crowd of 86,520 cheered the Bulldogs to their first 6-0 start since 1982, the last time Georgia had won an SEC championship. Michael McCarter/AJC

consecutive running plays. Kicker Phillip Newman attempted a 44-yard field goal to give the Vols a 3-2 lead, but Georgia linebacker Boss Bailey leaped high in the air to block it.

"I got up higher than I would to dunk a basketball on that," said Bailey, who has a 46-inch vertical jump.

The Bulldogs got the ball back at their 47-yard line and got to Tennessee's 13 after quarterback David Greene completed three passes in a row. But Georgia had to settle for Billy Bennett's 27-yard field goal, which gave the Bulldogs a 5-0 lead with 3:58 left in the second quarter.

On the last play of the first half, Bennett kicked a 44-yard field goal to give Georgia an 8-0 lead.

The Volunteers drove deep into Georgia territory on the opening possession of the second half. The Volunteers faced fourth-and-1 at Georgia's 29, but junior defensive end Shedrick Wynn sacked Banks for a 16-yard loss.

"I was looking for a bootleg run," Wynn said. "I was just there to get it. It was exciting to make a big play like that. That gave us a lot of momentum."

The Bulldogs scored the game's first touchdown on their next possession. On third-and-6, Brown caught an 11-yard touchdown pass from Greene just inside the goal line. Bennett's extra point made it 15-0 with 8:27 remaining in the third quarter.

Georgia added another field goal after Banks fumbled the snap at Tennessee's 39-yard line. Freshman nose tackle Kedric Golston recovered the ball at the Vols' 36, and Bennett kicked a 47-yard field goal four plays later for an 18-0 lead.

Things got a little hairy for Georgia in the fourth quarter. With 11:52 remaining in the game, Banks threw a screen pass to Derrick Tinsley, who broke loose for a 33-yard touchdown. Banks was stopped short of the end zone on the two-point conversion try, and the Bulldogs held an 18-6 lead.

	1st	2nd	3rd	4th	Final
TENNESSEE	0	0	0	13	13
GEORGIA	2	6	10	0	18

SCORING SUMMARY

QTR	TEAM	PLAY		TIME
1st	Georgia	SFT	Team safety	3:50
2nd	Georgia	FG	Bennett 27-yd. field goal	3:58
2nd	Georgia	FG	Bennett 44-yd. field goal	0:02
3rd	Georgia	TD	Brown 11-yd. pass from Greene (Bennett kick)	8:27
3rd	Georgia	FG	Bennett 47-yd. field goal	5:53
4th	Tennessee	TD	Tinsley 33-yd. pass from Banks (2-pt. conv. fails)	11:52
4th	Tennessee	TD	Witten 5-yd. pass from Tinsley (Newman kick)	3:21

OFFENSE

TENNESSEE

PASSING	ATT	COMP	INT	YDS	TD
Banks	15	10	0	168	1
Leak	3	1	0	9	0
Tinsley	1	1	0	5	1

RECEIVING	CATCHES	YDS	TD
Washington	3	32	0
Brown	2	57	0
Tinsley	2	34	1
Fleming	1	26	0
Riggs Jr.	1	10	0
Davis	1	9	0
Scott	1	9	0
Witten	1	5	1

RUSHING	RUSHES	YDS	TD
Davis	14	65	0
Banks	14	35	0
Tinsley	3	32	0
Riggs	3	10	0
Wade	1	17	0
Washington	1	10	0
Fleming	1	4	0
Leak	3	-11	0

GEORGIA

PASSING	ATT	COMP	INT	YDS	TD
Greene	37	22	1	232	1

RECEIVING	CATCHES	YDS	TD
Edwards	7	112	0
Johnson	4	37	0
Gary	2	30	0
Watson	4	26	0
Brown	1	11	1
Wall	1	6	0
Smith	2	8	0
Gibson	1	2	0

RUSHING	RUSHES	YDS	TD
Smith	19	29	0
Milton	5	26	0
Wall	3	15	0
Greene	2	-2	0

Georgia's offense picked up three first downs on its next series, but the Bulldogs were forced to punt from the Volunteers' 36. Tennessee got the ball back at its 20 and put together its best drive of the game.

On third-and-20 from the Vols' 47, Banks completed a 39-yard pass to receiver Kelley Washington to the Georgia 8. On third-and-goal, Tinsley threw a halfback pass to tight end Jason Witten, who beat two defenders for a touchdown. Newman's extra point was good, and suddenly, the Vols had cut Georgia's lead to 18-13 with 3:21 remaining.

The Volunteers tried an onside kick, but Georgia senior safety Burt Jones recovered the ball at Tennessee's 43. Bulldogs running back Tony Milton was stuffed for no gain on third-and-2, and Richt faced another critical call. With Georgia facing fourth-and-2 at Tennessee's 35 with 1:43 left, the textbook decision might have been to punt and try to pin the Vols deep in their territory.

Instead, Richt went for the first down. Milton took a toss from Greene and burst 25 yards around the right end to the Volunteers' 10.

"I wasn't nervous at all," Greene said. "We run that play all the time. It would have been different if it was a play we'd just drawn up."

The call was nothing new for Richt, who had been second-guessed throughout his two seasons at Georgia for his play calling late in the game.

"Coach has nerves of steel," Stinchcomb said.

And with that, the Bulldogs started looking ahead to the second half of the season.

"We've got a chance to be great," Greene said. "We've beat some good teams and still haven't played our best ball."

LEFT:
Billy Bennett's second field goal gave the Bulldogs an 8-0 lead. He had three in the game. Brant Sanderlin/AJC

ABOVE:
Sophomore Reggie Brown's blocked punt on Tennessee's Dustin Colquitt led to a safety, Georgia's first points of the game. Brant Sanderlin/AJC

AGE: 20

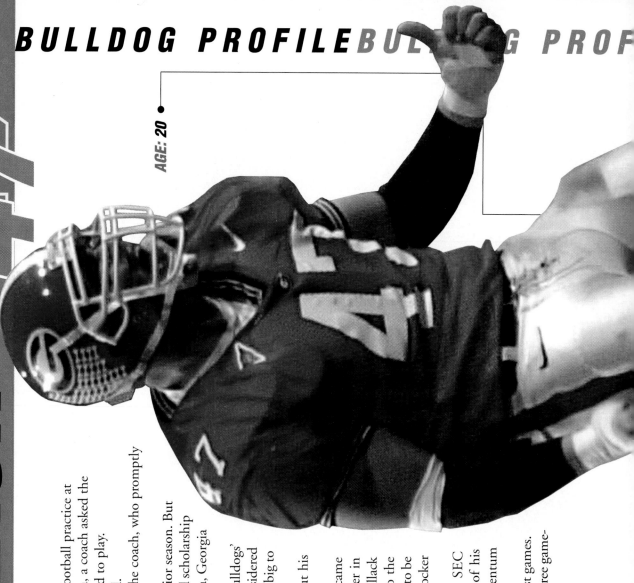

DAVID POLLACK

47

When David Pollack reported for his first football practice at Shiloh High School in suburban Atlanta, a coach asked the stubby freshman what position he wanted to play.

"Fullback and linebacker," Pollack said.

"Not at that weight and speed," said the coach, who promptly put Pollack on the offensive line.

Pollack didn't make Shiloh High's varsity squad until his junior season. But as a senior, he was among the state's most recruited players and had scholarship offers from more than a dozen colleges, including Florida, Georgia, Georgia Tech, Ohio State and South Carolina.

Even after Pollack signed to play football at Georgia, the Bulldogs' coaching staff was unsure which position he'd play. Pollack was considered too small to play on the defensive line in the SEC, but perhaps too big to play fullback.

Two years later, Pollack has answered all the questions about his abilities as a football player.

His 14 sacks broke the Georgia single season record, and he became the first Bulldogs sophomore since running back Herschel Walker in 1981 to be named to the Associated Press' All-America first team. Pollack also was a finalist for the Bronko Nagurski Award, which goes to the nation's top defensive player, and became the first defensive player to be named SEC Player of the Year since Auburn defensive tackle Tracy Rocker in 1988.

"Some of the plays he made, without them, we're not SEC champions," coach Mark Richt said. "He didn't get it because of his reputation going into the season. He really didn't have any momentum for awards like this going into the season."

Pollack provided some of the biggest plays in Georgia's biggest games. In the 13-7 victory at South Carolina on Sept. 14, Pollack made three game-

HOMETOWN: **SNELLVILLE, GA.**

CLASS: **SOPHOMORE**

Brant Sanderlin/AJC

DEFENSIVE END

changing plays, including a touchdown interception in which he plucked the ball out of the hand of Gamecocks quarterback Corey Jenkins as he threw from the South Carolina end zone. Pollack also recovered a fumble at Georgia's 2-yard line and forced another when the Gamecocks were driving for a go-ahead touchdown in the final minute.

Pollack blocked a field goal in the win at Alabama and had two sacks in the Bulldogs' 18-13 victory over Tennessee. In the Bulldogs' 20-13 loss to Florida, he intercepted a pass inside Georgia's 5-yard line and returned it 39 yards. Pollack also lined up at fullback for the game-clinching run against Clemson in the opener.

"We thought we had a guy who was a good athlete, who was going to be a team guy and who was a hard worker," Richt said. "He was a dominating player in that [South Carolina] game, there's no question. Is he going to be a dominating player throughout his career? I wouldn't be surprised because what you saw in that game is what we see in practice every day."

Indeed, Pollack's teammates and coaches said his best attributes are his work ethic and attitude. Pollack joined Shiloh High's wrestling team as a junior and eventually wrestled as Shiloh's heavyweight because the team didn't have one. He had a 36-8 record and finished second in the Class AAAA state wrestling tournament, even though most of his opponents were 20 pounds heavier.

"He believed in himself when maybe nobody else did," said Steve Hassenger, his wrestling coach in high school.

Pollack's teammates also say he might be Georgia's most determined player. When he was moved from defensive tackle to end this past spring, Richt said Pollack resembled a "fish out of water." In his first season at the position, however, Pollack led the SEC with 14 sacks, 36 quarterback pressures and 23 tackles for loss.

"You just make so many more plays [when you hustle]," Pollack said. "I guess that's why I do it. If I can't go full-speed to the ball, I'll take myself out. It's not how many plays you play, it's how hard you go on every play. You're not guaranteed tomorrow. You might as well bust it on every play."

Pollack, 20, said that attitude was instilled in him by his father, Norm Pollack, who coached him in youth football. Pollack and Georgia quarterback David Greene were the stars on the Shiloh youth team that won five consecutive Gwinnett County championships, from ages 8 to 12.

"His mouth or his motor are always running," Norm Pollack said. "Something is going to be moving. If you watch him on the sideline, he's never standing still. He's always moving."

South Carolina found out how fast Pollack moves on the field. On the Gamecocks' final drive, which ended with running back Andrew Pinnock's fumble at the Georgia 5, South Carolina used three offensive tackles to try to block Pollack. None succeeded.

"That's quite a compliment," Richt said.

SATURDAY, OCTOBER 19, 2002
GEORGIA 48, VANDERBILT 17

SAILING TO 7-0

Bulldogs score on first eight possessions in easy victory

ATHENS, Ga. — Vanderbilt usually waits until it gets to the stadium to wreck.

But some of the Commodores were bruised and battered before they even arrived at Sanford Stadium to play in Georgia's homecoming game. One of Vanderbilt's buses was involved in an accident on the way to the stadium. Fortunately, there weren't any serious injuries — until kickoff.

With Georgia fans fearing a letdown after emotional victories over Alabama and Tennessee, the No. 5-ranked Bulldogs scored on their first eight possessions — six touchdowns, two Billy Bennett field goals — to raise their record to 7-0 for the first time since 1982.

Georgia ran up 606 yards of total offense, the most since the Bulldogs had 667 against Southern Mississippi in 1993. The Bulldogs opened the game with touchdown drives of 79, 80 and 92 yards and didn't punt until there were only eight minutes left.

"I'm relieved," Georgia coach Mark Richt said. "I'm relieved we didn't lay an egg. I'm relieved that we came out and played really hard. And I'm very relieved that our offense came out and started looking like we'd hoped they would."

Quarterback David Greene looked smart after his performance against the Commodores. He completed his first 10 passes and finished 20-for-23 for 319 yards and two touchdowns. He also scored on an 11-yard run in the third quarter.

"It feels great," Greene said. "Probably for a whole game, as far as completions and attempts, that was my best game at Georgia."

On the first play of the second quarter, Richt called "44-Flatback-Rooskie," a trick play that worked against Auburn last season. Greene faked a handoff to tailback Musa Smith, who faked a run off the left guard. As Vanderbilt defenders converged on Smith, Greene hid the ball and turned his back to the line of scrimmage.

Down the field, Bulldogs receiver Terrence Edwards slowed down to fake a block on free safety Jonathan Shaub. Shaub, who made a perfect score of 1,600 on the SAT, bit on the fake and left Edwards alone behind the secondary. Greene delivered a perfect pass to Edwards, who scored on a 65-yard touchdown to give the Bulldogs a 14-7 lead with 14:48 left in the first half.

"I saw that SAT score in the newspaper this morning," Edwards said. "That play makes me feel a lot smarter."

Greene didn't throw an incompletion until Edwards dropped a pass on the right sideline with 6:41 left in the first half. Greene threw only two incompletions in the first half, and the other one was a pass over the middle to Damien Gary, which could have been called pass interference against Vanderbilt.

"Greene was on point today," said Georgia receiver Reggie Brown, who caught one pass for 20 yards. "We exploited their weaknesses, and he put it on the money."

RIGHT:
Freshman Tyson Browning, eluding Vanderbilt's Rushen Jones, played the most he had all season, catching two passes for 20 yards and running four times for 17 yards. Brant Sanderlin/AJC

ABOVE:

David Greene did it all against the Commodores, including running for an 11-yard touchdown in the third quarter.

Brant Sanderlin/AJC

Greene got off to such a fast start that Richt abandoned his plan of playing backup quarterback D.J. Shockley in the first two quarters. Shockley, who hadn't played since breaking his left foot at South Carolina on Sept. 14, entered the game on Georgia's third series of the second half and didn't show much rust from a four-game layoff.

Shockley completed 7 of 9 passes for 94 yards, including a 9-yard touchdown to tight end Ben Watson to give the Bulldogs a 48-17 lead with 14:16 left. Shockley also rushed for 4 yards on four carries.

"It felt really good," Shockley said.

Richt wasn't feeling very good about his team's injury situation after the game. Georgia avoided the injury bug the first half of the season but was faced with some serious concerns. Two starters — Smith and receiver Fred Gibson — suffered thumb injuries and would miss at least one game. Also, offensive tackle Jon Stinchcomb missed most of the game with a sprained left knee.

"We're banged up pretty good," Richt said. "I thought going into the game we'd been very fortunate [to avoid injuries]. Pregame warmups took their toll on some guys."

Still, Richt was relieved his team didn't overlook the Commodores, who last spoiled Georgia's homecoming in 1994. With a road game against Kentucky and a showdown against Florida in Jacksonville looming on the schedule, it would have been easy for the Bulldogs to look past Vanderbilt.

"Some teams look past these types of games," said Edwards, who had seven receptions for 163 yards and a touchdown. "But these seniors weren't going to let that happen. If we'd lost, we'd have been in a dogfight to go to Atlanta."

Instead, the Bulldogs moved a step closer to playing in their first SEC championship game.

"We're still not getting the recognition that a top-five team deserves," Georgia running back Tony Milton said.

	1st	2nd	3rd	4th	Final
VANDERBILT	7	3	7	0	17
GEORGIA	7	24	10	7	48

SCORING SUMMARY

QTR	TEAM	PLAY		TIME
1st	Georgia	TD	Gibson 35-yd. pass from Greene (Bennett kick)	5:22
1st	Vanderbilt	TD	Cutler 1-yd. run (Johnson kick)	2:23
2nd	Georgia	TD	Edwards 65-yd. pass from Greene (Bennett kick)	14:48
2nd	Georgia	TD	Smith 14-yd. run (Bennett kick)	8:24
2nd	Georgia	FG	Bennett 32-yd. field goal	4:06
2nd	Georgia	TD	Smith 1-yd. run (Bennett kick)	0:51
2nd	Vanderbilt	FG	Johnson 46-yd. field goal	0:00
3rd	Georgia	FG	Bennett 30-yd. field goal	10:42
3rd	Georgia	TD	Greene 11-yd. run (Bennett kick)	8:05
3rd	Vanderbilt	TD	Doster 9-yd. run (Johnson kick)	2:38
4th	Georgia	TD	Watson 9-yd. pass from Shockley (Bennett kick)	14:16

OFFENSE

VANDERBILT

PASSING	ATT	COMP	INT	YDS	TD
Cutler	20	10	0	158	0

RECEIVING	CATCHES	YDS	TD
Stricker	5	109	0
Garrett	2	49	0
Doster	2	5	0
Smith	1	-5	0

RUSHING	RUSHES	YDS	TD
Doster	15	118	1
Cutler	13	63	1
Bourque	9	33	0
Tant	5	18	0
Stricker	1	1	0
Cola	1	1	0

GEORGIA

PASSING	ATT	COMP	INT	YDS	TD
Greene	23	20	0	319	2
Shockley	9	7	0	94	1
Phillips	2	1	0	13	0

RECEIVING	CATCHES	YDS	TD
Edwards	7	163	1
Watson	5	50	1
Smith	3	31	0
Gary	3	17	0
McClendon	2	42	0
Milton	2	23	0
Browning	2	20	0
Gibson	1	35	1
Brown	1	20	0
Raley	1	16	0
Johnson	1	9	0

RUSHING	RUSHES	YDS	TD
Smith	14	102	2
Wall	3	27	0
Milton	8	21	0
Browning	4	17	0
Shockley	4	4	0
Snyder	2	4	0
Brown	1	3	0
Greene	5	2	1

**" SOME TEAMS LOOK PAST THESE TYPES OF
GAMES. BUT THESE SENIORS WEREN'T GOING
TO LET THAT HAPPEN. IF WE'D LOST, WE'D HAVE
BEEN IN A DOGFIGHT TO GO TO ATLANTA. "**

— RECEIVER TERRENCE EDWARDS

ABOVE:
The Georgia defense gave up 392 total yards but held the Commodores to 17 points and none in the fourth quarter. Brant Sanderlin/AJC

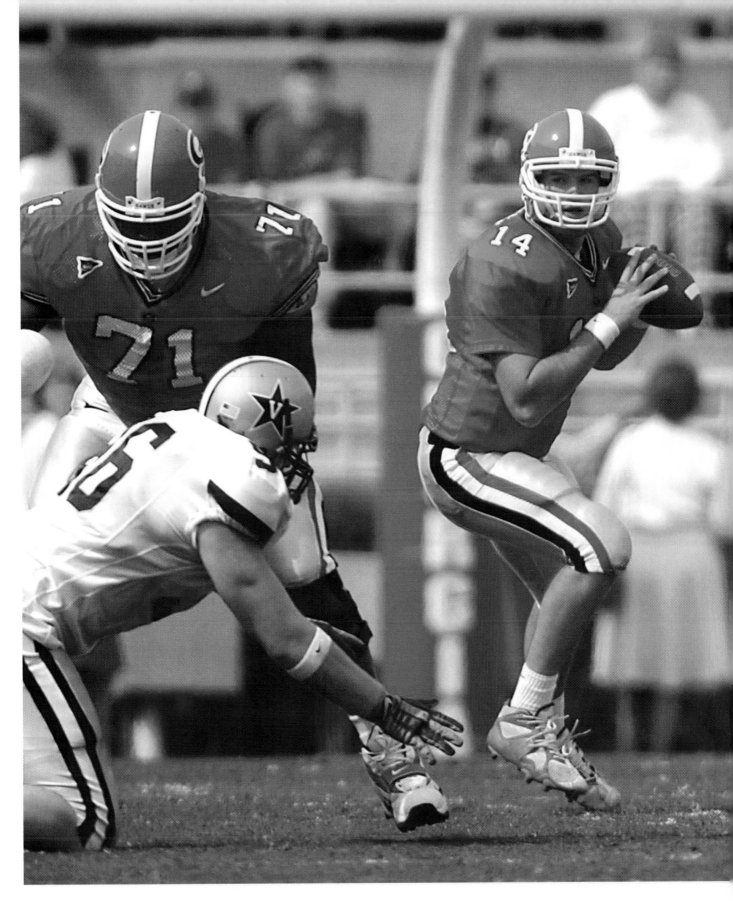

ABOVE:
David Greene faked out the Vanderbilt defense to connect with Terrence Edwards (right) on a 65-yard pass that gave Georgia a 14-7 lead. The touchdown was part of a 24-point second quarter. Brant Sanderlin/AJC

ABOVE:
The Bulldogs' convincing victory did not come without a price. Fred Gibson scored Georgia's first touchdown, but he would miss the next two games with a thumb injury. *Brant Sanderlin/AJC*

LEFT:
Musa Smith leaves defenders grasping for air as he gains a chunk of his 102 rushing yards in the 48-17 victory against Vanderbilt. Brant Sanderlin/AJC

SATURDAY, OCTOBER 26, 2002
GEORGIA 52, KENTUCKY 24

"GOAL-POST MOMENT?"

Bulldogs squash Kentucky's party plans with dominating second half

LEXINGTON, Ky.—Georgia arrived in Kentucky with the local newspaper declaring the game a "goal-post moment" for the Wildcats.

But the only thing falling at Commonwealth Stadium were Georgia records and Jared Lorenzen, the Wildcats' 300-pound quarterback.

Bulldogs quarterback David Greene tied a school record with four touchdown passes, and backup D.J. Shockley passed for two touchdowns in the No. 5-ranked Bulldogs' 52-24 win. Their six touchdown passes set a school record.

Greene and Shockley outpassed Lorenzen 353 yards to 208. Georgia's offense produced 529 yards and 33 first downs, the third-highest total for first downs

in school history. The Bulldogs scored 100 points in consecutive victories over Vanderbilt and Kentucky.

"I was hoping it would be like that," coach Mark Richt said of his two-quarterback system. "I was hoping both quarterbacks would play well and do their own things. They've got two different styles, and they're both good leaders. I was hoping those guys would both play well on the same day, and they've done that the past two weeks."

Next for Georgia was a showdown in Jacksonville against Florida, which had beaten the Bulldogs in 11 of the previous 12 meetings. Georgia would clinch the SEC East and their first appearance in the SEC championship game if they could beat the Gators.

"There was not a huge celebration, and I think it's because we know what's ahead of us," Richt said. "We know how good Florida is and how good they've been against Georgia. We still haven't done anything yet in the SEC East."

In the first half, it seemed that the Wildcats might get to tear down their goal posts after the game. Kentucky stormed

BELOW:
D.J. Shockley and David Greene combined for a record-setting day, but there wasn't a huge celebration because they knew Florida was next on the schedule. Brant Sanderlin/AJC

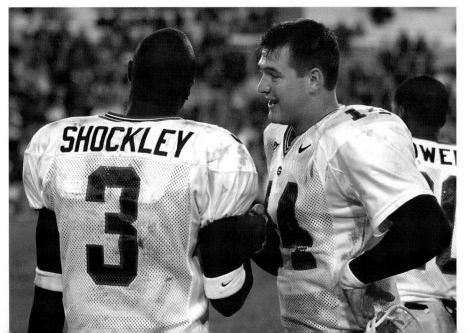

RIGHT:
The Georgia defense, including David Pollack (47), Tony Gilbert and Ken Veal (96) didn't allow Kentucky to score in the second half despite allowing 24 first-half points. Brant Sanderlin/AJC

D.J. Shockley ran for 38 yards in addition to passing for 102 and throwing for two touchdowns. Brant Sanderlin/AJC

to a 24-21 halftime lead, with Lorenzen throwing touchdowns of 24 yards to Aaron Boone and 60 yards to Derek Abney. The Wildcats gained more than 250 yards in the first half.

At halftime, though, Georgia linebackers Tony Gilbert and Boss Bailey reminded their teammates what was at stake.

"We were missing too many tackles and blowing too many assignments," Gilbert said. "We were doing a lot of things that helped Kentucky score. We knew what we needed to do, but they just needed to hear it from somebody."

Whatever Georgia's star linebackers said seemed to turn things around. After rushing for 102 yards and a touchdown on 14 carries in the first half, Kentucky's Artose Pinner was stuffed for 9 yards on five attempts in the second half. Lorenzen also didn't find much room, throwing for 34 yards on 5-for-10 passing after halftime.

Most important, the Wildcats were shut out in the final 30 minutes.

"We made some adjustments to some things we should have been doing right from the beginning," Georgia defensive coordinator Brian VanGorder said. "We kind of sat out there like ducks in the first half and gave up the big plays."

But only Georgia's offense was making big plays in the second half. Even with star running back Musa Smith, receiver Fred Gibson and offensive tackle Jon Stinchcomb sidelined with injuries, the Bulldogs scored on their first three possessions after halftime. Greene threw a 41-yard touchdown to Terrence Edwards on the first drive and then found Edwards again for a 12-yard touchdown to give the Bulldogs a 35-24 lead with 10:25 left in the third quarter.

Shockley came back into the game on Georgia's next possession and drove the offense 83 yards in 11

	1st	2nd	3rd	4th	Final
GEORGIA	14	7	21	10	52
KENTUCKY	17	7	0	0	24

SCORING SUMMARY

QTR	TEAM	PLAY		TIME
1st	Kentucky	TD	Pinner 33-yd. run (Begley kick)	12:37
1st	Georgia	TD	Gary 25-yd. pass from Greene (Bennett kick)	10:18
1st	Kentucky	TD	Boone 24-yd. pass from Lorenzen (Begley kick)	8:53
1st	Georgia	TD	Watson 15-yd. pass from Shockley (Bennett kick)	4:24
1st	Kentucky	FG	Begley 24-yd. field goal	0:10
2nd	Georgia	TD	Edwards 12-yd. pass from Greene (Bennett kick)	13:34
2nd	Kentucky	TD	Abney 60-yd. pass from Lorenzen (Begley kick)	6:21
3rd	Georgia	TD	Edwards 41-yd. pass from Greene (Bennett kick)	12:28
3rd	Georgia	TD	Edwards 12-yd. pass from Greene (Bennett kick)	10:25
3rd	Georgia	TD	Gary 8-yd. pass from Shockley (Bennett kick)	2:25
4th	Georgia	FG	Bennett 26-yd. field goal	9:17
4th	Georgia	TD	Powell 1-yd. run (Bennett kick)	0:56

OFFENSE

GEORGIA

PASSING	ATT	COMP	INT	YDS	TD
Greene	32	16	0	251	4
Shockley	14	10	1	102	2
Edwards	1	1	0	4	0

RECEIVING	CATCHES	YDS	TD
Watson	6	68	1
Gary	6	62	2
Edwards	5	127	3
Brown	5	52	0
Wall	2	22	0
Johnson	1	13	0
Browning	1	9	0
Shockley	1	4	0

RUSHING	RUSHES	YDS	TD
Milton	18	78	0
Shockley	6	38	0
Powell	7	23	1
Wall	3	16	0
Greene	5	11	0
Browning	1	6	0

KENTUCKY

PASSING	ATT	COMP	INT	YDS	TD
Lorenzen	27	13	0	208	2
Boyd	4	2	0	34	0

RECEIVING	CATCHES	YDS	TD
Boone	5	88	1
Abney	4	99	1
Cook	2	24	0
Harp	2	23	0
Gaffron	1	6	0
Kamphake	1	2	0

RUSHING	RUSHES	YDS	TD
Pinner	19	111	1
Boyd	2	36	0
Bwenge	1	-4	0
Lorenzen	8	-13	0

ABOVE:
More than 70,000 fans watched the Bulldogs improve to 8-0.
Brant Sanderlin/AJC

"As long as we're scoring points, it doesn't matter to me," Greene said. "It's a team game. You could see today that it worked pretty well for both of us."

Kicker Billy Bennett, who was sickened with salmonella all week, started the game and made seven PATs and a 26-yard field goal. Bennett said he got sick after eating a Caesar salad after the Vanderbilt game and lost five pounds leading up to the Kentucky game. Bennett declined to name the restaurant where he ate.

"I didn't even know there were eggs in Caesar salad," Bennett said. "I guess they're in the dressing or something. They'll be hearing from the health department."

Redshirt freshman Tony Milton, making his first career start in place of Smith, rushed for 78 yards and leveled safety Mike Williams with a block on one of Greene's touchdown passes to Edwards. It was Milton's first start in four years. The former high school All-American from Tallahassee, Fla., was out of football for two years after he signed with Syracuse but failed to qualify academically. Milton briefly lived out of his car while working as a caterer at a hotel.

"I made mistakes, and I'm going to have to go Monday and correct them," Milton said. "I wish I'd gotten 100 yards, but I can't complain."

Richt wasn't complaining after Milton helped the Bulldogs gain 172 rushing yards.

"I think he is one tough son of a gun," Richt said. "I am so happy that he is on this team and out of the situation he was in with his life. He started a game for Georgia on national television and played big. I am very happy for him."

Milton said he hoped the team's performance would help critics realize that Georgia was a legitimate contender in the SEC race.

"For some reason, people don't believe in Georgia," Milton said. "It's like they think we're a fluke."

The Bulldog Nation would wait until the Florida game to make its assessment.

plays. His 8-yard touchdown to junior Damien Gary gave Georgia a 42-24 lead.

"We both got the job done," Shockley said. "Whoever is in there, he's going to get the job done. This is what we've been looking for, and this is how we expected this thing to work."

Greene, who completed 16 of 32 passes for 251 yards, said he didn't mind watching Shockley perform from the sideline.

RIGHT:
"We both got the job done," D.J. Shockley, being tackled by Morris Lane, said of his and David Greene's performances. Brant Sanderlin/AJC

THERE WAS NOT A HUGE CELEBRATION, AND I THINK IT'S BECAUSE WE KNOW WHAT'S AHEAD OF US. WE KNOW HOW GOOD FLORIDA IS AND HOW GOOD THEY'VE BEEN AGAINST GEORGIA. WE STILL HAVEN'T DONE ANYTHING YET IN THE SEC EAST.

— BULLDOGS COACH MARK RICHT

ABOVE:
The offense scored on its first three possessions of the second half, the first two coming on passes of 41 and 12 yards from David Greene to Terrence Edwards to give the Bulldogs a 35-24 lead. Brant Sanderlin/AJC

BOSS BAILEY

45

AGE: 23

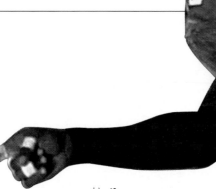

It's nearly 10 a.m. on a Wednesday, and Boss Bailey has missed his first tackle all season.

Bailey's 2-year-old son, Khalil, scrambles across the living room of their two-bedroom apartment, reluctant to get dressed for preschool. Boss Bailey, 23, already has been awake for more than three hours. About 7 a.m., he waited in the rain for a bus that carried him across town to attend the first of his three sociology classes.

An hour and a half later, Bailey is back home to feed and dress his son. But Khalil is excited about an unfamiliar visitor and is unwilling to finish his eggs and sausage.

Just after 10 a.m., Bailey and his wife, the former Amber Knight, make a short drive to the Athens YWCO, where Khalil attends preschool. After a brief goodbye, the couple drives closer to campus and boards a bus. They each have two more hours of classes.

After their last class ends at 1:10 p.m., the couple returns to their apartment for lunch. Boss gets some brief down time, knowing that the hectic part of his schedule has yet to begin. The Bulldogs begin meetings at 2:30 p.m. Practice starts at 3:30 and usually lasts more than two hours.

"We handle it," Boss says. "It's not always easy, but we just try to be patient. It's not going to be something that lasts forever."

But this year has been the best of times for Bailey, the Bulldogs' star linebacker. He helped Georgia win its first SEC championship in 20 years and was named to the All-America team. He will likely be a first-round pick in next spring's NFL draft, making him a multimillionaire. More importantly, Khalil is healthy and has shown no ill effects from two heart surgeries he underwent shortly after birth.

Boss and Amber Bailey, a 22-year-old native of Cartersville, Ga., met at a Georgia basketball game about four years ago. Boss proposed to her last summer, and they were married about a month later at a chapel in Helen, Ga. — during the football team's first open weekend Sept. 22.

Brant Sanderlin/AJC

CLASS: SENIOR

HOMETOWN: FOLKSTON, GA.

LINEBACKER

"It takes a strong person to be able to handle football and academics," offensive tackle Jon Stinchcomb says. "To add a wife and child to that, and to see how Boss handles that responsibility, I've got the utmost respect for him."

But Bailey says he feels fortunate, not frenzied. Khalil was born with a heart defect on June 30, 2000. Soon after coming home from the hospital, Khalil was having trouble breathing, his lips turning blue. He was rushed to the emergency room and hospitalized in intensive care. A week later, Khalil was transferred to Children's Healthcare of Atlanta at Egleston, where doctors diagnosed the heart problem.

When Khalil was 17 days old, he underwent four hours of heart surgery to reimplant his left coronary artery. Doctors weren't sure he would make it out of surgery. But Khalil did, and he recovered from another surgery last August to repair a microvalve problem in his heart.

Now, the only reminder of his past health problems is a scar on his chest.

"You'd never look at him and think he's had two heart surgeries," Amber Bailey says. "He's active. I think he has a high pain tolerance."

Initially, Boss worried that his son wouldn't be as active as other children and couldn't play sports. Boss is the third son of Elaine and Roland Bailey to play football at Georgia. Older brothers Ronald and Champ were starting cornerbacks. Boss says he hopes that his son will one day play for the Bulldogs, too.

And Khalil already is showing the traits of a linebacker — he recently was scolded at preschool for tackling classmates by the ankles.

"At first, they said Khalil couldn't play football or sports, but based on his recent checkups, I think he'll be able to do whatever he wants," Boss Bailey says.

About 6 p.m. almost every day, Amber and Khalil wait for Boss outside Georgia's locker room. Boss' football duties are finally over, but his day isn't done. He goes home to feed and bathe Khalil. The couple finally gets some quiet time when Khalil goes to bed about 9 p.m. An hour later, they're in bed, waiting to start another day.

"Boss handles it all pretty well," Amber says. "Some days are better than others. I admire him for being able to do it all. I don't think I could do it."

SATURDAY, NOVEMBER 2, 2002
FLORIDA 20, GEORGIA 13

ANOTHER FLORIDA HANGOVER IN JACKSONVILLE

Bulldogs sputter at cocktail party, fall to Gators for 12th time in 13 years

JACKSONVILLE, Fla.—What was supposed to be the biggest party in years turned into another Florida hangover for the Bulldogs.

After losing to nemesis Florida 20-13 in Jacksonville's Alltel Stadium, Georgia had the weary look of losers for the first time. But the Bulldogs had no time to mourn. If Georgia was going to salvage what it hoped would be a championship season, it had to regroup quickly.

After their first loss of the season, the No. 5-ranked Bulldogs needed to beat Ole Miss at home and Auburn on the road in its final two conference games to win the SEC's Eastern Division. That would earn the Bulldogs their first trip to the SEC championship game in Atlanta's Georgia Dome.

"We've got to look at the big picture," quarterback David Greene said. "If we win our next two games, we're champions of the SEC East. This is disappointing. We felt we had a real good shot this year. We've got to bounce back. It's just one loss. We've still got control of our own destiny."

Georgia would have won the SEC East with a victory over the Gators. But after losing to Florida for the 12th time in 13 meetings, Georgia couldn't afford to lose either of its last two SEC games. A combination of one Georgia loss and two Florida victories would have put the Gators back into the championship game.

"It's hard to swallow," Bulldogs tailback Musa Smith said. "But it's not like it's the end of our season.

There are still great things ahead for us. We shot ourselves in the foot. We didn't take advantage of the things the defense set up for us. We had our defense on the field too long. We just didn't do what we prepared to do. But it's not like our season's over."

Against the Gators, Georgia didn't look anything like the team that had captured the imagination of the Bulldog Nation during the first nine weeks of the season. The Bulldogs were 0-for-13 on third down. They had two turnovers, inexcusable penalties and dropped passes. Georgia seemed like a team overwhelmed by what was at stake.

"You never want to predict that you'll play like we did," Bulldogs coach Mark Richt said. "It's very disappointing that we didn't put on a better show. We had some opportunities."

For the first time in a decade, former Florida coach Steve Spurrier's large shadow didn't hover over the Bulldogs. Georgia felt this year was its best shot at beating the Gators, who were under fire after early-season losses to Ole Miss and LSU. But Gators first-year coach Ron Zook and his staff drew up an unpredictable game plan. They hit Georgia's defense with quick screen passes, controlling the clock and keeping the Bulldogs' offense off the field.

RIGHT:
During his four seasons, Terrence Edwards had broken almost all of Georgia's receiving records, but that didn't seem to matter to fans after he dropped a pass that could have sent the game into overtime. Rich Addicks/AJC Staff

Of Gators quarterback Rex Grossman's career-high 36 completions against the Bulldogs, 18 of them came on screen passes. Florida gained 108 of its 339 passing yards off screens.

Georgia's offense came into the game having scored 100 points in consecutive victories over Vanderbilt and Kentucky. The Bulldogs jumped ahead of Florida 7-0 on their second possession and seemed ready to light up the scoreboard again. But the offense sputtered, and the passing game was sporadic with top receivers Damien Gary and Fred Gibson sidelined with injuries.

The Bulldogs had their opportunities. Sophomore receiver Reggie Brown fumbled inside Florida territory. Greene fumbled after guard Alex Jackson knocked the ball out of his hand. Defensive end David Pollack's handoff to safety Sean Jones after an interception was ruled a forward lateral. Backup quarterback D.J. Shockley threw an interception that safety Guss Scott returned for a touchdown. The Bulldogs were penalized for an illegal shift on second-and-goal at Florida's 2-yard line. All those miscues happened in the first half.

"We all made mistakes today," Georgia offensive tackle Jon Stinchcomb said.

The Bulldogs' frustration continued in the second half. On Florida's second possession of the third quarter, Grossman threw a throwback screen to tailback Earnest Graham. Cornerback Bruce Thornton hit him, Graham fumbled, and defensive tackle Darrius Swain recovered

	1st	2nd	3rd	4th	Final
FLORIDA	0	12	0	8	20
GEORGIA	7	6	0	0	13

SCORING SUMMARY

QTR	TEAM	PLAY		TIME
1st	Georgia	TD	Wall 10-yd. pass from Greene (Bennett kick)	6:59
2nd	Florida	TD	Walker 5-yd. pass from Grossman (PAT fails)	9:39
2nd	Florida	TD	Scott 47-yd. interception return (2-pt. conv. fails)	3:56
2nd	Georgia	FG	Bennett 47-yd. field goal	1:20
2nd	Georgia	FG	Bennett 25-yd. field goal	0:03
4th	Florida	TD	Troupe 10-yd. pass from Grossman (2-pt. conv. good)	11:32

OFFENSE

FLORIDA

PASSING	ATT	COMP	INT	YDS	TD
Grossman	46	36	2	339	2

RECEIVING	CATCHES	YDS	TD
Perez	12	76	0
Kight	9	115	0
Walker	4	64	1
Troupe	4	47	1
Graham	3	17	0
Small	2	8	0
Jackson	1	9	0
Sharp	1	3	0

RUSHING	RUSHES	YDS	TD
Graham	18	40	0
Carthon	9	23	0
Grossman	4	-8	0
Brown	1	-9	0

GEORGIA

PASSING	ATT	COMP	INT	YDS	TD
Greene	29	11	0	141	1
Shockley	6	3	1	27	0

RECEIVING	CATCHES	YDS	TD
Watson	4	21	0
Edwards	3	63	0
Brown	2	46	0
Wall	2	17	1
Milton	2	6	0
Johnson	1	15	0

RUSHING	RUSHES	YDS	TD
Smith	22	100	0
Milton	5	40	0
Shockley	3	13	0
Wall	1	1	0
Greene	5	-28	0

at Florida's 19. The Bulldogs gained 2 yards on their first two plays, and then Greene threw incomplete.

The Bulldogs would have faced a 35-yard field-goal attempt, but offensive tackle George Foster was penalized 15 yards for a personal foul against linebacker Bam Hardmon. Georgia kicker Billy Bennett's field-goal attempt, now from 50 yards, hit the left upright.

"My emotions got out," Foster said. "I wasn't provoked. I just lost my cool."

Bennett missed another field goal, this one from 36 yards, on the Bulldogs' next possession. Georgia had

driven to the Florida 19 for a first down, but went no farther.

The Bulldogs' last gaffe will be the one that is remembered most by Georgia fans. With the Bulldogs trailing 20-13, they took possession at their 33-yard line with 2:31 left. On first down, receiver Terrence Edwards got behind the Gators' secondary after a defensive back slipped on the turf. Greene threw a perfect pass to Edwards at about the Florida 35, but Edwards dropped what might have been the game-tying touchdown. There wasn't another player around him for 10 yards.

ABOVE:
Musa Smith, Terrence Edwards (right) and the Bulldogs got off to a good start after J.T. Wall, center, caught a 10-yard pass from David Greene to give the Bulldogs a 7-0 lead. Brant Sanderlin/AJC

ABOVE:

Terrence Edwards didn't have much time to dwell on his costly dropped pass. Shortly after the game, he was on his way to the hospital to be with his mother, Jeannette, who had collapsed in the stands. She was released after spending three days in a Florida hospital. Brant Sanderlin/AJC

"You hate to see the game come down to one play like that," Richt said. "The game wasn't won or lost with that play. It would have helped, though."

Three plays later, Georgia lost the ball on downs. The Bulldogs got it back one more time with 36 seconds left, but that wasn't enough time to put together a scoring drive.

"Oh, man," said Thornton, who watched Edwards drop the pass from the sideline. "He made a beautiful move on No. 9 [Scott]. Terrence catches that ball 10 out of 10 times in practice. I know he thinks he should have made that catch."

Worse, Edwards learned after the game that his mother, Jeannette, had collapsed in the stands. Some of Edwards' teammates consoled him before he left for the hospital.

"We told him to keep his head up," linebacker Tony Gilbert said. "The last thing we need is for him to have his head down, thinking he lost the game."

Said Stinchcomb: "You lick your wounds for 24 hours. You lie in bed for a day with the covers over your head and think about it. But you have to realize we still hold our destiny in our hands. There are bigger fish to fry."

ABOVE:
Despite all of their success during the previous eight games, Ian Knight (56) and the rest of the Bulldogs could not find a way to beat the Gators. Brant Sanderlin/AJC

FOLLOWING PAGE:
Florida's Keiwan Ratliff upends Tony Milton, who can't make the catch during the fourth quarter, and the Gators hand the Dogs their only loss of the season in Jacksonville.

Brant Sanderlin/AJC

SATURDAY, NOVEMBER 9, 2002

GEORGIA 31, MISSISSIPPI 17

REBELLION

Bulldogs blast Ole Miss to move closer to Georgia Dome

ATHENS, Ga. — And the magic number was one.

After defeating Ole Miss 31-17 in Sanford Stadium, the No. 7-ranked Bulldogs were in position to clinch the SEC East and a spot in the SEC championship game with a victory over Auburn. A loss to the Tigers and a Florida victory over South Carolina would send the Gators to Atlanta.

"How much bigger can next week get?" Bulldogs defensive end David Pollack asked. "You're playing for the SEC East and a chance to go to the Georgia Dome. It doesn't get any bigger than that."

The Bulldogs showed no signs of a hangover from their 20-13 loss to Florida. Georgia gained 402 yards

of total offense, and its defense shut out Ole Miss in the second half, the second time during the season the Bulldogs had held an opponent scoreless in the final 30 minutes.

"It was huge," Georgia coach Mark Richt said. "Any game you win in this league is a big win. It puts us in position to get a second chance, which you don't get often. I know it's unusual to get a second chance like we're getting. Hopefully, the guys will take advantage of it and do something special."

A Georgia victory over the Rebels seemed easy from the outset, but then again, nothing had been easy for the Bulldogs. Sophomore receiver Fred Gibson, back from a two-game absence because of a thumb injury, returned the opening kickoff 44 yards to the Bulldogs' 48-yard line. Georgia converted a third-and-8 at the 50, and then quarterback David Greene connected with senior Terrence Edwards for a 21-yard pass to the Rebels' 20. Five plays later, senior fullback J.T. Wall pushed in for a 1-yard touchdown and a 7-0 lead with 11:18 left in the first quarter.

But Ole Miss and quarterback Eli Manning came back. Manning completed his first three passes for 44 yards, and then the Rebels moved to Georgia's 11 on a pass-interference penalty. Two plays later, tailback Tremaine Turner scored on an 8-yard run to tie the game at 7.

On Georgia's next possession, Greene was intercepted by safety Wes Scott, who returned the ball

BELOW:
Robert Geathers had one of two sacks against Eli Manning. For the second time in three games, the defense held its opponent scoreless in the second half. Brant Sanderlin/AJC

RIGHT:
Tremaine Turner led Ole Miss with 89 yards on 19 carries and scored the Rebels' two touchdowns. Brant Sanderlin/AJC

ABOVE:
Musa Smith ran a career-high 37 times for 148 yards. He had gained 100 or more yards in six of the first 10 games.
Brant Sanderlin/AJC

to the Bulldogs' 31. Ole Miss converted a pair of first downs to move to Georgia's 4, but the Bulldogs held and forced the Rebels into a 19-yard field-goal attempt. Georgia linebacker Boss Bailey leaped high to block Jonathan Nichols' attempt, and the Bulldogs took over at their 6. It was Bailey's second blocked field goal of the season.

"The blocked field goal was just huge," Richt said. "That just shows the heart of this team, to push through like that to block the field goal. That was a big, big momentum play for us."

On the opening possession of the second quarter, the Rebels faced third-and-8 at Georgia's 44. Manning threw to the left flat for Bill Flowers, but freshman cornerback Tim Jennings intercepted the pass and returned it 64 yards for a touchdown. Billy Bennett's extra-point kick gave the Dogs a 14-7 lead with 13:09 left in the first half.

"Georgia did a good job of utilizing the zone blitz," said Manning, who threw for only 176 yards on 12-for-25 passing. "It was a new blitz that we had not seen.

I wasn't accounting for [Jennings], and I threw it right to him."

Ole Miss tied the game at 14 on Turner's 1-yard run with 4:58 left in the first half. The Bulldogs went back on top 21-14 with less than two minutes left in the half when Greene found Gibson for a 17-yard touchdown. Gibson caught the ball near the right hash mark, spun right to break cornerback Travis Blanchard's tackle and beat Scott to the end zone.

Nichols kicked a 24-yard field goal with 26 seconds left in the half, cutting Georgia's lead to 21-17 at halftime.

In the second half, Georgia went ahead 24-17 on Bennett's 40-yard field goal with 4:16 left in the third quarter. The Bulldogs got another touchdown on their next possession, with Greene throwing a 33-yard touchdown to Edwards, making it 31-17.

Georgia's defense held the Rebels to two first downs on their first four possessions of the second half. After cornerback Bruce Thornton broke up Manning's long pass to receiver Taye Biddle on third-and-9 with

	1st	2nd	3rd	4th	Final
MISSISSIPPI	7	10	0	0	17
GEORGIA	7	14	10	0	31

SCORING SUMMARY

QTR	TEAM	PLAY		TIME
1st	Georgia	TD	Wall 1-yd. run (Bennett kick)	11:18
1st	Mississippi	TD	Turner 8-yd. run (Nichols kick)	8:13
2nd	Georgia	TD	Jennings 64-yd. interception return (Bennett kick)	13:09
2nd	Mississippi	TD	Turner 1-yd. run (Nichols kick)	4:58
2nd	Georgia	TD	Gibson 17-yd. pass from Greene (Bennett kick)	1:49
2nd	Mississippi	FG	Nichols 24-yd. field goal	0:26
3rd	Georgia	FG	Bennett 40-yd. field goal	4:16
3rd	Georgia	TD	Edwards 33-yd. pass from Greene (Bennett kick)	1:41

OFFENSE

MISSISSIPPI

PASSING	ATT	COMP	INT	YDS	TD
Manning	25	12	2	176	0

RECEIVING	CATCHES	YDS	TD
Collins	4	38	0
Johnson	2	62	0
Razzano	2	11	0
Flowers	1	26	0
Turner	1	16	0
Armstead	1	15	0
Fryfogle	1	8	0

RUSHING	RUSHES	YDS	TD
Turner	19	89	2
Jacobs	4	16	0
McClendon	4	7	0
Razzano	2	4	0
Manning	3	-9	0

GEORGIA

PASSING	ATT	COMP	INT	YDS	TD
Greene	22	12	1	206	2

RECEIVING	CATCHES	YDS	TD
Edwards	5	90	1
Gibson	4	97	1
McClendon	1	18	0
Wall	1	9	0
Milton	1	-8	0

RUSHING	RUSHES	YDS	TD
Smith	37	148	0
Milton	8	23	0
Wall	4	17	1
Shockley	2	10	0
Greene	2	0	0

ABOVE:

Fresh from his victory in the Georgia governor's race, Sonny Perdue spent some time with coach Mark Richt and the Bulldogs. Brant Sanderlin/AJC

about 11 minutes left in the game, the Rebels were forced to punt. Ole Miss never got the ball back.

The Bulldogs took over at their 20 and ran 17 times in 19 plays to eat up the final 10 minutes, 46 seconds. Junior running back Musa Smith carried 13 times during the final drive.

"We didn't seem to have the ball that much in the second half," Ole Miss coach David Cutcliffe said. "It was hard to watch the last 10 minutes."

Smith ran a career-high 37 times for 148 yards against the Rebels, the sixth game in which he had gained 100 yards or more. Smith needed 138 yards in the final two regular-season games to become Georgia's first 1,000-yard rusher since Garrison Hearst in 1992. Georgia ran 54 times against the Rebels, the highest total in Richt's two seasons.

"I was a little tired at the end," Smith said. "I never thought I'd get that many. I didn't even know I got 37 carries. I never even got 37 carries in high school."

"Musa is running very hard," Richt said. "He had a lot of big runs. He didn't have any real long runs, but he made some nice cuts, broke some tackles and kept going for yards after contact. This is his best game since I've been here, as far as him being 'the man' and grinding out tough yards."

The victory proved costly for the Bulldogs. Edwards, who caught five passes for 90 yards, separated his left shoulder on an incomplete pass on the first play of the fourth quarter. He was expected to miss three to six weeks. The Bulldogs already were playing without junior Damien Gary, who wasn't expected back until after the regular season because of a torn muscle in his leg. Gibson played with a cast on his left hand because of an injured thumb.

"We've really gotten banged up at the receiver position," Richt said. "Some other guys have got to step up."

ABOVE:
Georgia's Terrence Edwards rebounded from the Florida game and had five catches for 90 yards and a touchdown against the Rebels. Brant Sanderlin/AJC

> *ANY GAME YOU WIN IN THIS LEAGUE IS A BIG WIN. IT PUTS US IN POSITION TO GET A SECOND CHANCE, WHICH YOU DON'T GET OFTEN. I KNOW IT'S UNUSUAL TO GET A SECOND CHANCE LIKE WE'RE GETTING. HOPEFULLY, THE GUYS WILL TAKE ADVANTAGE OF IT AND DO SOMETHING SPECIAL.*

— BULLDOGS COACH MARK RICHT

ABOVE:
The Bulldogs got some words of encouragement from Gov.-elect Sonny Perdue. *Brant Sanderlin/AJC*

RIGHT:
Fred Gibson wore a cast on his injured left thumb that forced him to miss two games, but it didn't seem to bother him much against Mississippi. He made four catches for 97 yards, scoring once, and returned kickoffs three times for 95 yards.
Brant Sanderlin/AJC

MUSA SMITH

When running back Musa Smith showed up at Georgia unannounced the summer before he became a high school senior, the first player he met was receiver Michael Johnson.

"Hey, man, you coming here to help us?" Johnson asked.

That made a positive impression on Smith.

"Everywhere else we'd been, the players looked at him like, 'Who are you? You're not taking my job,'" said Kevin Zakis, one of two high school assistant coaches who took Smith on a cross-country tour of colleges. "Musa asked Michael Johnson where he was from, and Johnson said Oklahoma. Musa was like, 'Oklahoma?' I think he was a little flabbergasted that a kid from Oklahoma could come to Georgia and fit in."

Smith was looking for a place to fit in, too. More and more, he's finding it.

He's a Muslim on a team whose coach expresses strong Christian beliefs. He's a Northerner in the South. But Smith, who said he always felt like a minority in his central Pennsylvania hometown of Elliottsburg, began to blend in as a junior at Georgia.

Teammates said Smith was more open this season after keeping to himself the past couple of seasons.

"I think he's getting a little closer to the team," senior linebacker Tony Gilbert said. "He talks to more people now. He was coming a long way from Pennsylvania. You might tend to be more quiet than other people when you've come that far."

Smith's family didn't have television, but Smith said it wasn't by choice. Because of mountains and hills that surrounded their farm, the Smiths could never get reception. Because of that, Smith knew very little about Georgia and its football program before he visited Athens.

"I was just a normal kid growing up in a small town," Smith said.

But his religion made him different.

"He was the only Muslim in our school," Zakis said.

When Georgia fired coach Jim Donnan two seasons ago and replaced him with Mark Richt, Smith had some concerns. But Smith said those concerns weren't about his new coach's strong Christian beliefs.

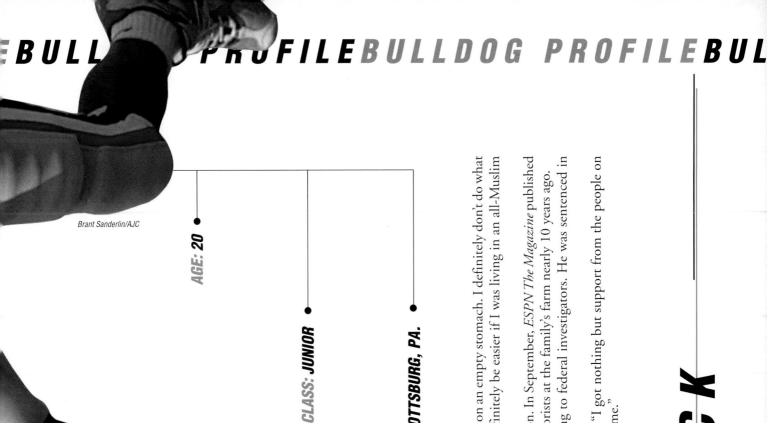

Brant Sanderlin/AJC

AGE: 20

CLASS: JUNIOR

HOMETOWN: ELLIOTTSBURG, PA.

TAILBACK

"My only concern was about him being from Florida State and being a quarterbacks coach," Smith said. "I was worried that we were going to have a big air attack."

But Smith has fit into Richt's offense. With 1,324 rushing yards this season, the Sugar Bowl MVP became the Bulldogs' first 1,000-yard rusher in 10 years. He also was named to the Associated Press' All-SEC first team, the first Georgia tailback to receive that honor since Garrison Hearst in 1992.

"Musa has really exceeded our expectations this year," Richt said.

Smith said his goals this year also included becoming a better Muslim. He started attending a mosque in Athens regularly. He prays five times daily.

During the past two seasons, Richt has taken his team to churches in Athens. Smith declines to go but attends chapel service on game days and also prays at midfield after games.

Smith, 20, said he struggles to balance football and his religion. Muslims are supposed to fast from sunrise to sunset during Ramadan, which fell between Nov. 6 and Dec. 6 this year.

"I can't fast," Smith said. "I'd die if I did. With the way we practice, I'd die if I went out there on an empty stomach. I definitely don't do what a true Muslim is supposed to do. It's a struggle because I live in a Christian society. It would definitely be easier if I was living in an all-Muslim society, but I'm not."

Earlier this year, Smith had to confront his family's past and tough questions about his religion. In September, *ESPN The Magazine* published a story about Smith and his father, Kelvin Smith, who court documents say trained Islamic terrorists at the family's farm nearly 10 years ago.

Kelvin Smith, also known as Abdul Muhaimin in court documents, was convicted of lying to federal investigators. He was sentenced in March 1999 to a year and one day in a federal prison.

His parents were worried for Musa's safety when the story was published, but, Smith said, "I got nothing but support from the people on campus and from the Bulldog Nation. It was really comforting. It made me feel like I was at home."

SATURDAY, NOVEMBER 16, 2002
GEORGIA 24 , AUBURN 21

DESTINY'S DOGS

"We're going to Atlanta;" late touchdown gives Georgia SEC East title

AUBURN, Ala.—The drought was over. After waiting 20 years for another championship, No. 7-ranked Georgia wrapped up the SEC's Eastern Division on an improbable play from an unlikely hero.

Junior receiver Michael Johnson, thrust into the starting lineup after injuries to Terrence Edwards and Damien Gary, scored the winning 19-yard touchdown with 85 seconds left in the Bulldogs' 24-21 victory over Auburn at Jordan-Hare Stadium.

On fourth-and-15, Johnson outjumped Tigers cornerback Horace Willis for the ball in the back of the end zone. The Bulldog Nation hasn't come down since.

"That's what is so great about this team," said Georgia athletics director Vince Dooley, who coached the Bulldogs to their last SEC championship in 1982. "They never quit. They just keep going and going."

BELOW:

With the SEC East championship on the line, coach Mark Richt remained outwardly calm despite a late-game interception by Auburn. He held out hope the defense could stop the Tigers.
W.A. Bridges Jr./AJC

Thanks to their stingy defense and Johnson, the Bulldogs would play for the SEC championship. After watching Florida and Tennessee play for the SEC title the past decade, the Bulldogs finally would get to play for a championship in their back yard.

"We talked in preseason camp about what it was going to take to knock the lid off this program," Georgia coach Mark Richt said. "For whatever reason, it seemed like there was a lid on the Georgia program, and we couldn't knock it off. We talked about what it was going to take to knock it off, and it was leadership."

The victory was a relief for the Bulldogs, who were forced to win their last two SEC games after losing to Florida 20-13.

"We're going to Atlanta," senior linebacker Tony Gilbert said. "We should have been there a long, long time ago."

That's exactly what Richt said he thought when he took the Georgia job two years ago. During

ABOVE:
The winning drive started at the Georgia 41 with 1 minute, 58 seconds left in the game. It ended 33 seconds later when David Greene lofted a pass to Michael Johnson, who jumped over Horace Willis in the back of the end zone. The Bulldogs were SEC East champions. Brant Sanderlin/AJC

ABOVE:
D.J. Shockley played sparingly and finished with minus-1 yards passing and minus-4 yards rushing. Brant Sanderlin/AJC

his 15 years as a Florida State assistant, Richt said he thought the Bulldogs' program was a sleeping giant. Under former coaches Ray Goff and Jim Donnan, the Bulldogs had the talent to win but always fell short in their best seasons. It looked like Richt's team also would falter.

The Bulldogs fell behind 21-10 late in the third quarter, and all hope seemed lost. But offensive tackle Jon Stinchcomb, of all players, scored a touchdown to pull Georgia back into the game. He fell on quarterback David Greene's fumble in the end zone, pulling the Bulldogs within 21-17 with 2:02 left in the third quarter.

In the fourth quarter, the Bulldogs twice got near midfield, but Johnson lost a fumble after a catch, and then Greene threw an interception at the Auburn 33. Georgia got as close as the Tigers' 29 with about 2:30 left, but the Bulldogs failed to convert on fourth down, and Auburn got the ball back.

Georgia's defense shut down the Tigers again, holding them without a first down for the fifth consecutive possession in the fourth quarter. The Tigers punted from their 38 with 2:11 left, and safety Sean Jones returned it 16 yards to the Georgia 41.

"Our defense came through down after down today," Richt said. "We did a fantastic job shutting Auburn down in the second half."

The Bulldogs still had to go 59 yards in less than two minutes. On first down, Greene threw a 4-yard pass to Johnson, who stepped out of bounds with 1:54

	1st	2nd	3rd	4th	Final
GEORGIA	3	0	14	7	24
AUBURN	7	7	7	0	21

SCORING SUMMARY

QTR	TEAM	PLAY		TIME
1st	**Auburn**	TD	Brown 53-yd. run (Duval kick)	6:29
1st	**Georgia**	FG	Bennett 43-yd. field goal	2:34
2nd	**Auburn**	TD	B. Johnson 2-yd. pass from Campbell (Duval kick)	1:40
3rd	**Georgia**	TD	Greene 1-yd. run (Bennett kick)	10:46
3rd	**Auburn**	TD	Campbell 21-yd. run (Duval kick)	5:45
3rd	**Georgia**	TD	Stinchcomb 1-yd. fumble recovery in end zone	2:02
4th	**Georgia**	TD	M.Johnson 19-yd. pass from Greene (Bennett kick)	1:25

OFFENSE

GEORGIA

PASSING	ATT	COMP	INT	YDS	TD
Greene	35	18	1	232	1
Shockley	3	1	0	-1	0

RECEIVING	CATCHES	YDS	TD
Johnson, M.	13	141	1
Gibson	4	72	0
Watson	1	19	0
Milton	1	-1	0

RUSHING	RUSHES	YDS	TD
Smith	15	90	0
Greene	10	13	1
Wall	3	9	0
Stinchcomb	0	1	1
Milton	2	-3	0
Shockley	2	-4	0

AUBURN

PASSING	ATT	COMP	INT	YDS	TD
Campbell	23	12	2	133	1

RECEIVING	CATCHES	YDS	TD
Johnson	4	45	0
Brown	2	33	0
Aromashodu	2	26	0
Smith	1	14	0
Wallace	1	9	0
Diamond	1	4	0
Johnson	1	2	1

RUSHING	RUSHES	YDS	TD
Brown	25	124	1
Campbell	19	72	1
Smith	2	3	0

ABOVE:
Naomi Duncan from Buford, Ga., didn't care that she was in a stadium filled with Tigers fans. She let the Bulldogs know she was there. Brant Sanderlin/AJC

left. On the next play, sophomore Fred Gibson got behind Willis and caught a 41-yard pass to the Auburn 14. Suddenly, the Bulldogs had new life. But Greene threw incomplete on first down, and then the Bulldogs were penalized 5 yards for a false start. On second-and-15, Greene's pass was batted down at the line. The Bulldogs appeared to miss their only opportunity to score when Greene overthrew tight end Ben Watson in the end zone with 1:31 remaining.

That's when all of Georgia's hopes and dreams of an SEC title came down to this: fourth-and-15 from the Auburn 19. The Bulldogs needed a miracle. On the sideline, Richt was unsure of what play to call.

"We had a different play that we'd been practicing all year long; we called that play 'Touchdown' because you've got to score on it," Richt said. "It seemed like every time we practiced it, I was standing there thinking there's no way we're going to be able to hold the ball long enough for this to work. Then I'd think: Maybe

[the quarterback] can scramble a little bit; maybe he can buy enough time.

"But when it got down to that moment of truth and it was time to call this play that we've been practicing all along, I was just afraid that there was no way [it'd work]. I felt like we got to have something else."

So Richt called "70-X-Takeoff," a play the Bulldogs hadn't used in a game all season and hadn't practiced in more than a month. Gibson streaked down the right side, with Johnson doing the same on the left. Greene pump-faked to Gibson and then lofted the ball to the left corner of the end zone. Willis slipped on the wet turf, and Johnson pulled it down by jumping over Willis.

"I thought I might have underthrown it a little bit," Greene said. "But our coaching staff preaches giving our guys a chance to catch the ball, so I didn't want to throw it too far. But that's what Michael gives

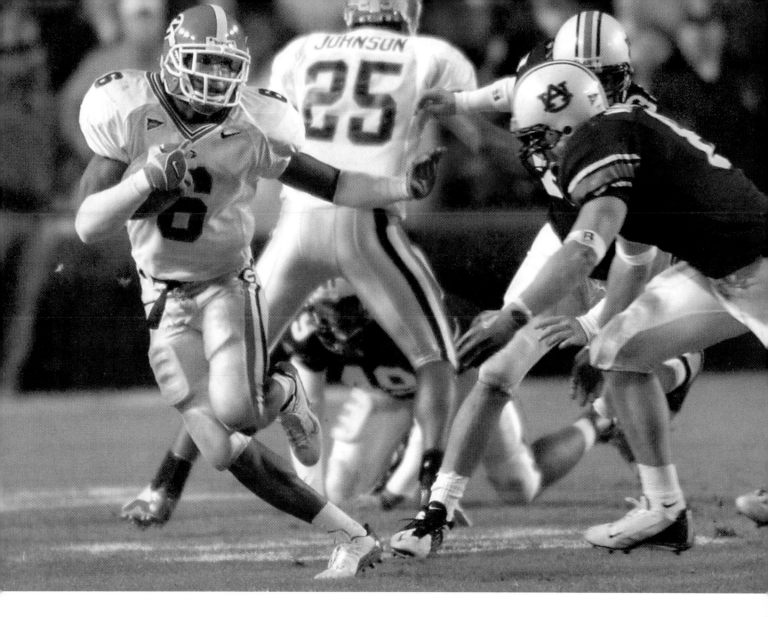

ABOVE:
Sean Jones gave the Bulldogs good field position for the winning drive after returning a punt 16 yards to the Georgia 41. Brant Sanderlin/AJC

us. You don't have to throw a perfect pass for him to catch it."

It was a defining moment for Johnson, a junior from Tulsa, Okla., who was used rarely in his first two seasons. But when Edwards separated his left shoulder against Ole Miss, Johnson was forced to start at Auburn. He caught a career-high 13 passes for 141 yards, including one of the biggest touchdowns in school history.

"Michael's the type of person who deserved that type of game," Edwards said. "He's been through a lot.

He's had to back up me, and I know coming out of high school, everybody wants to play. And to be behind somebody who's already established himself like I had, he deserved that game."

After a 20-year wait, the Bulldogs would tell you that they deserved it, too.

"It's so hard to believe," senior linebacker Boss Bailey said. "It came down to the last game. We had to get it done. It couldn't have been any better. This is the sweetest."

ABOVE:
David Greene didn't have his best game, but it was good enough to lead the Bulldogs to victory.
Brant Sanderlin/AJC

LEFT:
"Our defense came through down after down," coach Mark Richt said of Tim Jennings and his teammates. "We did a fantastic job of shutting Auburn down in the second half." *Brant Sanderlin/AJC*

" *IT'S SO HARD TO BELIEVE, IT CAME DOWN TO THE LAST GAME. WE HAD TO GET IT DONE. IT COULDN'T HAVE BEEN ANY BETTER. THIS IS THE SWEETEST.* **"**

— SENIOR LINEBACKER
BOSS BAILEY

ABOVE:

It was a long wait, but Georgia fans, who aren't afraid to show their support, were rewarded with an SEC championship and a victory in the Sugar Bowl.
W.A. Bridges Jr./AJC

MARK RICHT

AGE: 42

Former Florida State assistant coach Chuck Amato still remembers his first game as North Carolina State's head coach.

"I looked around and realized I was all by myself," Amato says. "I was like, 'Where's Bobby?'"

Georgia coach Mark Richt probably had that same feeling in his first season away from Florida State, but Richt earned his wings in his second season, leading the Bulldogs to their first SEC championship in 20 years. In two seasons at Georgia, Richt has taken his team where some Bulldogs fans wondered if they would go again.

"For me to leave FSU, there had to be a higher calling than just winning games or making money," says Richt, who spent 15 years as a Seminoles assistant. "I just had a sense that it was time to jump out of the nest and fly out from under Coach Bowden's wing."

After a rookie season that included close losses and questionable coaching decisions, Richt has been fully embraced by the Bulldog Nation. His teams have beaten rivals Georgia Tech and Tennessee in each of the past two seasons. Although Georgia lost to Florida two more times, at least the Bulldogs were competitive in doing so.

But it's Richt's personality and leadership that have Georgia fans most excited. After a plethora of off-field problems sullied former coach Jim Donnan's final season, Richt cleaned up the Bulldogs' act. He suspended players who tripped up and instituted a character-building program, believed to be the only one of its kind in major college football.

"I told people, 'I don't care if this team goes 2-10 — he's building the program the right way,'" says Bob Kelly, a player on Georgia's 1980 national championship team. "There's no foul play. What he says is the gospel."

Richt, 42, is a devout Christian and makes no secret of his faith. During pre-season camp the past two seasons, he took his players to different churches in the Athens area. His brother-in-law, Kevin Hynes, is the team's chaplain. The team attended the chris-

Brant Sanderlin/AJC

HEAD COACH

HOMETOWN: **BOCA RATON, FLA.** •

ALMA MATER: MIAMI, FLA. (1982) •

tening of defensive coordinator Brian Van Gorder's youngest son and built a Habitat for Humanity home for a needy family.

Richt credits Bowden for his strong faith. Richt was a graduate assistant at Florida State in 1986 when a Seminoles player was shot and killed. The next day, Bowden addressed the team and asked each of his players and coaches if they were living righteously. Richt stepped forward and devoted himself to Christianity. After Florida State lost to Tennessee 23-16 in the 1999 Fiesta Bowl, Richt vowed to prove his obedience to God. He fasted for 40 consecutive days on nothing but water and fruit juices. He lost 32 pounds.

Georgia defensive tackle Darrell Holmes knows Richt's faith is genuine. When Holmes considered quitting the team last year, Richt pulled him aside in practice.

"Since I may never see you again," Richt told him, "I want to ask you one question: Where do you want to spend eternity?"

"It proved to me that he's very concerned about me as a person," Holmes says. "It made me really think about the consequences of what I was planning to do. It made me think that God had a purpose for me, and His purpose for me was to be here playing football and getting an education. Coach Richt let me know that quitting wasn't the right thing to do."

Holmes was back at practice the next day and has been at every one since.

Four years ago, Richt and his wife, Katharyn, were in church in Tallahassee, Fla., when their Sunday school class discussed caring for all of God's children. The Richts were so moved by the sermon that they decided to adopt a son, Zach, now 6, from an orphanage in the Ukraine. When they went to pick up Zach, they met Anya, a young girl born with birth defects. They brought both children home to live with their biological sons, David, 8, and Jon, 12.

"We always questioned whether [becoming a head coach] would be good for our family," Katharyn Richt says. "In this profession, whether you're an assistant coach or head coach, there is always going to be a lot of demands. On the flip side, it's a profession where the family can be involved. We can go to the practices and games, and the kids can see the outcome of his hard work."

Richt says his family helps him keep things in perspective.

"People may not want to hear it, but there are an awful lot of more important things in life than football," Richt says. "As important as it is to me, at what cost do you want to be successful? There are a bunch of coaches out there who sacrificed everything to be a head coach. They left their families and their lives behind."

SATURDAY, NOVEMBER 30, 2002

GEORGIA 51, GEORGIA TECH 7

TECH WRECKED

Bulldogs hand rival worst loss in 95-game series

ATHENS, Ga. — Here's how far Georgia has come under coach Mark Richt in two seasons: Two season earlier, the Bulldogs trailed Georgia Tech 27-3 at halftime. It was such an embarrassment that Georgia president Michael Adams was moved to fire coach Jim Donnan.

This season, the Bulldogs were beating the Yellow Jackets 34-0 at halftime. Georgia rolled Georgia Tech 51-7, the largest margin of victory in the 95-game history of the series. The offensive explosion couldn't have come at a better time for the No. 5-ranked Bulldogs, who would play Arkansas the following week for the SEC championship.

"It's good to finally perform," senior offensive tackle Jon Stinchcomb said. "Even after we clinched the SEC East, we were still talking about untapped potential. We still believe our best games are ahead of us."

After the Tech victory and Oklahoma State's upset of No. 4 Oklahoma earlier in the day, Georgia clung to the possibility that a victory over Arkansas in the SEC championship game and a Virginia Tech upset of No. 1 Miami could put the Bulldogs in the Fiesta Bowl, where they would play for the national championship.

"That's a little extra incentive," Richt said. "We all hope to have a shot. This game [SEC championship] is big enough on its own, but in the back of your mind, you've got to know that there is a chance that we could go to the Fiesta. It won't be the focus of our motivation because we all know Georgia hasn't won an SEC championship in 20 years. That's enough motivation

in itself, without question, but I'm sure everyone will be listening."

Regardless of the outcome of the Miami game, Georgia still had plenty at stake against Arkansas. The Bulldogs could win their first SEC championship since 1982 and become the first Georgia team since the 1980 national champions to win 12 games in a season.

"The workweek starts again," Stinchcomb said. "We seem to go back-to-back-to-back with big games, but that's the way we wanted it. We wanted to be in this position."

Against the Yellow Jackets, the Bulldogs scored on their first four possessions and six of the first eight. The Bulldogs had 552 yards of total offense against a Tech defense that had allowed 34 points in one game all season. Georgia had 322 passing yards on 17 completions and had almost a 14-minute advantage in time of possession.

"It's been a long time since we've been able to dominate a game like we did," said quarterback David Greene, who threw for 205 yards on 10-for-14 passing.

Yellow Jackets coach Chan Gailey, in his first season at Tech, was at a loss for words after one of the most embarrassing losses in school history.

"I obviously didn't get these guys ready to play," Gailey said. "It was a very poorly played game in all phases. At halftime, we talked about pride and

RIGHT:
Mario Raley and the Bulldogs capped the regular season in style by running up 51 points on the rival Yellow Jackets. W.A. Bridges Jr./AJC

ABOVE:
In what was a common sight during the game, Musa Smith dragged Jackets Jeremy Muyres (left) and Cory Collins on one of his 20 runs. Smith finished with 121 yards and one touchdown and became the first back since Garrison Hearst in 1992 to reach 1,000 yards in a season. Brant Sanderlin/AJC

execution. We asked them what they wanted to do: quit or play. The loss hurts."

Even Richt, who ended Georgia's three-game losing streak to Tech with a 31-17 victory in Atlanta last season, was surprised by his team's dominating performance.

"It looked like every facet of the team played about as good as we could play in the first half," Richt said. "I never would have predicted it to happen like that. ... Somehow, our guys just played lights-out."

Georgia Tech took the opening kickoff, picked up one first down and was forced to punt. Bulldogs safety Sean Jones returned the punt 79 yards for an

apparent touchdown, but the score was wiped out by a holding penalty. Georgia took over at its 20-yard line, and tailback Musa Smith gained 22 yards on his first carry. The theme for the rest of the game was set. After Greene threw a 17-yard pass to senior Terrence Edwards to the Tech 22, Smith scored five plays later on a 1-yard run for a 7-0 lead.

The Yellow Jackets got the ball back and were stuffed for no gain on third-and-1 to force a punt. The Bulldogs drove to Tech's 16 but were forced to settle for Billy Bennett's 46-yard field goal and a 10-0 lead with 2:29 left in the first. Tech punted again on its next possession, and backup quarterback D.J. Shockley

	1st	2nd	3rd	4th	Final
GEORGIA TECH	0	0	0	7	7
GEORGIA	10	24	10	7	51

SCORING SUMMARY

QTR	TEAM	PLAY		TIME
1st	**Georgia**	TD	Smith 1-yd. run (Bennett kick)	8:30
1st	**Georgia**	FG	Bennett 46-yd. field goal	2:29
2nd	**Georgia**	TD	Shockley 8-yd. run (Bennett kick)	12:37
2nd	**Georgia**	TD	Gibson 49-yd. pass from Greene (Bennett kick)	9:36
2nd	**Georgia**	FG	Bennett 30-yd. field goal	4:28
2nd	**Georgia**	TD	Wall 18-yd. run (Bennett kick)	2:57
3rd	**Georgia**	TD	Wall 2-yd. run (Bennett kick)	5:46
3rd	**Georgia**	FG	Bennett 30-yd. field goal	3:50
4th	**GT**	TD	J. Smith 4-yd. pass from Suggs (Manget kick)	14:46
4th	**Georgia**	TD	Browning 19-yd. run (Bennett kick)	4:19

OFFENSE

GEORGIA TECH

PASSING	ATT	COMP	INT	YDS	TD
Suggs	27	14	2	158	1
Bilbo	7	3	0	52	0
Smith, J.	2	1	0	12	0

RECEIVING	CATCHES	YDS	TD
Glover	5	62	0
Watkins	5	61	0
Thomas	4	63	0
Foschi	1	12	0
Daniels	1	10	0
Sampson	1	10	0
Smith, J.	1	4	1

RUSHING	RUSHES	YDS	TD
Smith, J.	3	47	0
Daniels	4	16	0
Clinkscale	5	13	0
Bilbo	5	11	0
Watkins	1	1	0
Eziemefe	1	0	0
Suggs	2	-7	0

GEORGIA

PASSING	ATT	COMP	INT	YDS	TD
Greene	14	10	0	205	1
Shockley	8	5	0	86	0
Phillips	3	2	0	31	0

RECEIVING	CATCHES	YDS	TD
Gibson	3	73	1
Johnson	3	68	0
Edwards	2	48	0
Watson	2	42	0
Brown	2	28	0
Raley	2	27	0
Galt	1	25	0
McClendon	1	9	0
Milton	1	2	0

RUSHING	RUSHES	YDS	TD
Smith, M.	20	121	1
Milton	8	39	0
Browning	7	29	1
Wall	3	22	2
Shockley	6	20	1
Powell	3	9	0
Thomas	4	4	0
Greene	4	-12	0

ABOVE:
Tony Milton and the Bulldogs ran for 230 yards rushing on 57 carries and scored five times on the ground. Brant Sanderlin/AJC

replaced Greene on the ensuing drive. On second-and-goal at the Tech 8, Shockley got loose around left end and scored for a 17-0 lead.

Georgia Tech drove into position for a 48-yard field goal midway through the second quarter, but linebacker Boss Bailey jumped high to block Luke Manget's kick. Georgia took over at its 28, and two plays later, Greene threw a 49-yard touchdown to sophomore Fred Gibson for a 24-0 lead.

Bennett added a 30-yard field goal to make it 27-0 with 4:28 left in the first half. Tech couldn't field the ensuing kickoff, and backup linebacker Derrick Holloway recovered the fumble at the Yellow Jackets' 26. Senior J.T. Wall scored on an 18-yard run three

plays later to give the Bulldogs a 34-0 lead with 2:57 left.

The Bulldogs scored three more times in the second half, and the Yellow Jackets got their only touchdown on quarterback A.J. Suggs' 4-yard pass to Jonathan Smith early in the third quarter.

"What better way to go out?" said Bailey, who blocked his third field goal of the season. "This is one of those senior classes that'll be remembered forever. Now, we definitely want to keep it rolling and keep winning. Each week is more important now."

And the next week would be the most important in years.

ABOVE:
Kerry Watkins and the Yellow Jackets finished with 222 yards passing against Bruce Thornton and the Bulldogs. But they only scored once, and that was early in the fourth quarter with Georgia leading 44-0. Brant Sanderlin/AJC

SANTA IS GIVING THE DAWGS A SUGAR BOWL

" WHAT BETTER WAY TO GO OUT?
THIS IS ONE OF THOSE SENIOR CLASSES
THAT'LL BE REMEMBERED FOREVER. NOW
WE DEFINITELY WANT TO KEEP IT ROLLING
AND KEEP WINNING. EACH WEEK IS
MORE IMPORTANT NOW. **"**

— BULLDOGS LINEBACKER BOSS BAILEY

BELOW:

Backups Tyson Browning (left) and Tim
Jennings made the most of their playing time.
Browning scored the Bulldogs' final touchdown,
and Jennings intercepted an A.J. Suggs pass
with time running out in the fourth quarter.
W.A. Bridges Jr./AJC

ABOVE:
With the game well in hand late in the fourth quarter, Georgia's David Pollack (left) and Musa Smith had some fun on the sideline. *Brant Sanderlin/AJC*

135

GEORGIA 30, ARKANSAS 3

HOG TIED

Bulldogs blow out Arkansas 30-3 to win SEC championship

ATLANTA — Georgia receiver Michael Johnson leaped into the first row of stands, hugging everyone in sight. Defensive tackle Ken Veal lay at midfield, openly weeping in joy. All the while, more than 60,000 Georgia fans stayed in their seats, chanting "S-E-C! S-E-C!" and "It's great ... to be ... a Georgia Bulldog!"

And who could blame them? After 20 years of frustration — two decades, for goodness sakes — the Bulldogs were football champions of the SEC after blasting Arkansas 30-3 in the Georgia Dome.

By becoming the second team in school history to win 12 games in a season — the other was the 1980 national championship team — the Bulldogs guaranteed themselves a spot in the Jan. 1 Sugar Bowl in New Orleans, where they likely would play ACC champion Florida State.

"It didn't really dawn on me that it was 20 years [since Georgia last won the SEC] until the beginning of the season, when we put our championship boards up," Georgia coach Mark Richt said. "I was shocked. I told our players, 'Let's change this. Let's knock this lid off the program.'"

Indeed, not since Herschel Walker was running between the hedges had the Bulldogs had that much to bark about.

"I can't explain it," Veal said. "I got all choked up out on the field when it was over. It still seems like I'm in a fog. I just know we did something very special."

Special? Georgia offensive tackle Jon Stinchcomb was in the locker room, talking on a cellular phone to his older brother Matt in California. Matt Stinchcomb was a two-time All-American at Georgia and is an offensive lineman with the Oakland Raiders. Matt Stinchcomb never got a chance to play for an SEC title.

"I was talking to him, telling him how great it feels," Jon Stinchcomb said. "I was like, 'You know how it feels after you win a big game like this.' He was like, 'No, I don't know how it feels.'"

The SEC championship game could have been even bigger, but top-ranked Miami beat Virginia Tech 56-45, dashing the Bulldogs' hopes of playing Ohio State for the national championship. Most of Georgia's players watched that game in their hotel rooms, and Richt worried that they might be dejected.

"It was pretty obvious that Miami was going to win at the beginning of the game," Georgia linebacker Boss Bailey said. "Miami took it to 'em. That's a lot better than it being a close game they pulled out at the end. After the first quarter, we put it behind us. We were like, 'Let's go win the SEC championship.'"

And Georgia easily took out 20 years of frustration on the Razorbacks. The Bulldogs stuffed Arkansas on its opening possession, with Bailey sacking Matt Jones for a big loss on third down. On fourth down, Georgia cornerback Decory Bryant flew in off the left flank and blocked Richie Butler's punt.

"We'd been practicing it all week because they've done it a lot this year," Butler said. "The only thing for me to do is to try and redirect it to the left, but the guy came in too fast and just jumped in front of it. If I

RIGHT:
David Greene ran for 17 yards, but it was his arm that won the game for Georgia. He was 17 of 29 for 237 yards and a touchdown. Rich Addicks/AJC

ABOVE:
Lawrence Richardson and the Razorbacks were defenseless against Fred Gibson (five catches for 93 yards) and the Bulldogs' passing attack. Brant Sanderlin/AJC

could have sped it up a little, I maybe could have got it off, but he just came flying in so quick. It's usually a delayed blitz, but it looked like he was on a dead sprint."

Bulldogs safety Burt Jones returned the blocked punt to the Hogs' 2-yard line, and tailback Musa Smith scored on the next play for a 7-0 lead.

Georgia fans, who filled an estimated 90 percent of the more than 74,000 seats, nearly blew the roof off the Georgia Dome.

"It was like a boom," Bulldogs receiver Terrence Edwards said. "I wasn't sure what happened."

Said Arkansas tailback Fred Talley: "We couldn't seem to rebound after that. That really kind of took us out of our game plan and had us trying to dig out of a hole the rest of the way."

The Razorbacks never recovered. Just over six minutes into the game, Smith scored again on a 17-yard run, giving the Bulldogs a 14-0 lead. It was 20-0

before the Razorbacks picked up a first down that didn't come from a Georgia penalty.

The Bulldogs scored on their first five possessions and led 23-0 at halftime. Georgia piled up 273 yards and 15 first downs in the opening half and held the Razorbacks to 74 yards.

"We came out to win the SEC championship," Stinchcomb said. "That was our goal all along. The way we came out and played showed how much we wanted it, too."

Bulldogs quarterback David Greene threw for 237 yards and a touchdown and was named the game's most valuable player. Greene threw a 20-yard touchdown to tight end Ben Watson in the fourth quarter to finish the scoring. Tailback Musa Smith rushed for 106 yards and two touchdowns, his eighth 100-yard game of the season, and Edwards caught seven passes for 92 yards.

	1st	2nd	3rd	4th	Final
GEORGIA	17	6	0	7	30
ARKANSAS	0	0	3	0	3

SCORING SUMMARY

QTR	TEAM	PLAY		TIME
1st	Georgia	TD	Smith 2-yd. run (Bennett kick)	11:58
1st	Georgia	TD	Smith 17-yd. run (Bennett kick)	8:49
1st	Georgia	FG	Bennett 29-yd. field goal	3:54
2nd	Georgia	FG	Bennett 42-yd. field goal	12:10
2nd	Georgia	FG	Bennett 39-yd. field goal	6:24
3rd	Arkansas	FG	Carlton 27-yd. field goal	0:52
4th	Georgia	TD	Watson 20-yd. pass from Greene (Bennett kick)	12:08

OFFENSE

GEORGIA

PASSING	ATT	COMP	INT	YDS	TD
Greene	29	17	0	237	1
Shockley	4	2	0	20	0

RECEIVING	CATCHES	YDS	TD
Edwards	7	92	0
Gibson	5	93	0
Brown	3	29	0
Wall	1	22	0
Watson	1	20	1
Milton	1	2	0
Smith	1	-1	0

RUSHING	RUSHES	YDS	TD
Smith	19	106	2
Greene	4	17	0
Milton	8	6	0
Browning	2	3	0
Wall	2	2	0
Shockley	1	-3	0

ARKANSAS

PASSING	ATT	COMP	YDS	INT	TD
Jones	17	9	60	0	0
Jackson	4	1	14	0	0

RECEIVING	CATCHES	YDS	TD
Smith	5	36	0
Birmingham	2	12	0
Hamilton	1	14	0
Wilson	1	10	0
Pierce	1	2	0

RUSHING	RUSHES	YDS	TD
Talley	17	51	0
Howard	3	14	0
Jones	9	12	0
Dickerson	2	7	0
Cobbs	1	2	0
Jackson	1	-4	0
Birmingham	1	-4	0
Poole	1	-13	0

ABOVE:
The Georgia defense led by Kedric Golston (left) and Robert Geathers (right) was the story of the championship after holding Fred Talley, a 1,000-yard rusher during the regular season, to 51 yards on 17 carries. W.A. Bridges Jr./AJC

RIGHT:
The Razorbacks weren't able to do anything through the air, either, as quarterback Matt Jones, tackled by Tony Gilbert (42) and David Pollack, was 9 of 17 for 60 yards. Rich Addicks/AJC

But the story of the night might have been Georgia's defense. Talley, a 1,000-yard rusher in the regular season, was held to 51 yards on 17 carries, and Jones managed only 12 yards on nine runs. Arkansas led the SEC in rushing offense with an average of 243 yards per game, but managed only 65 against Georgia. Jones didn't do anything through the air, either, completing nine of 17 passes for only 60 yards.

"I felt like they were playing with 12 [defenders] most of the night," Arkansas coach Houston Nutt said. "They have got a good team with very few weaknesses, if any. Our game is not to come from behind. Our game, as you know, is getting ahead, eat up the clock, use the clock and take care of the ball. They were geared up and did a great job on defense."

Afterward, Richt couldn't help but stay on the field and watch his players celebrate.

"It was fun to be there and to be in the show, so to speak," he said. "When it was over, to see the fans stay in the stands and enjoy it and watch the players have fun was an experience I'll never forget."

It was a night the Bulldog Nation won't forget any time soon, either.

RIGHT:
Defensive lineman Ken Veal basked in the championship glow of the Georgia Dome.
W.A. Bridges Jr./AJC

BELOW:
Michael Johnson leaped into the stands as more than 60,000 fans chanted "S-E-C! S-E-C!" after the Bulldogs ended 20 years of SEC championship futility.
Rich Addicks/AJC

ABOVE:
Matt Jones could not avoid the Georgia rush led by Chris Clemons, jumping on David Pollack's back. Jones was sacked three times, once by Pollack. Brant Sanderlin/AJC

ABOVE:
David Greene was named SEC championship game MVP, and coach Mark Richt later was recognized as SEC coach of the year. Rich Addicks/AJC

RIGHT:
Ben Watson scored the Bulldogs' final touchdown on a 20-yard pass from Greene. W.A. Bridges Jr./AJC

WEDNESDAY, JANUARY 1, 2003

GEORGIA 26, FLORIDA STATE 13

SUGAR HIGH

Bulldogs' defense, special teams too much for undermanned Seminoles

NEW ORLEANS — What might be the second-best season in modern Georgia football history ended just as the greatest one did — with a victory in the Sugar Bowl.

And like Georgia's 1980 national champions, the 2002 edition of the Bulldogs used a sound running game, stingy defense and outstanding special teams to beat No. 16-ranked Florida State 26-13 in the Louisiana Superdome.

Bulldogs running back Musa Smith ran for 145 yards and was named the game's most outstanding player, kicker Billy Bennett kicked four field goals, and Georgia's defense forced three turnovers against the short-handed Seminoles.

The victory capped a memorable season for the Bulldogs, who won 13 games for the first time, won their first Southeastern Conference championship in 20 years and would finish in the top five of the Associated Press poll for the first time since 1983.

"It was a glorious season and it's a big step," Georgia coach Mark Richt said. "In the locker room, we were happy, but we didn't act like it's the first time we've won a big game. The players are learning how to win, expecting to win. That's a great sign."

The No. 4-ranked Bulldogs were expected to beat the Seminoles, who were playing without starting quarterback Chris Rix and defensive tackle Darnell Dockett, who were suspended from playing in the game because of off-field problems. Florida State finished 9-5, the first time the Seminoles had lost five games in a season since 1981.

"It's the kind of season where you're glad it's over," Florida State coach Bobby Bowden said. "I'm glad it's over."

The Seminoles, an eight-point underdog, still mustered a good fight against the Bulldogs. Bennett, a junior, gave Georgia a 3-0 lead with a 23-yard field goal on the Bulldogs' first drive. But after safety Kentrell Curry intercepted FSU quarterback Fabian Walker's pass and returned it to the Seminoles' 34-yard line, the Bulldogs were stuffed on offense. Bennett's 47-yard field-goal attempt was partially deflected and sailed wide left.

Florida State got the ball back at its 31-yard line, and two penalties against the Bulldogs moved the ball to Georgia's 33. Four plays later, Walker threw a 5-yard touchdown pass to junior Anquan Boldin. Xavier Beitia's extra point gave the Seminoles a 7-3 lead with 13 minutes, 41 seconds left in the first half.

The Seminoles looked ready to go ahead 14-3 after Georgia quarterback D.J. Shockley fumbled on a run on his first play of the game. The Seminoles drove to Georgia's 34-yard line, but Walker was hit as he threw into the right flat. Cornerback Bruce Thornton stepped in front of running back Willie Reid, intercepted the pass and returned it 71 yards for a touchdown. Bennett's extra point gave the Bulldogs a 10-7 lead with 6:24 left in the half.

ABOVE:
Musa Smith and the Bulldogs were pumped up to win their first Sugar Bowl championship since the 1980 team.
Michael McCarter/AJC

ABOVE:
Terrence Edwards, David Greene, Fred Gibson and the Georgia offense took a 17-7 lead into the second half.
Curtis Compton/AJC

"I saw the quarterback get flushed out of the pocket, and it looked like he was trying to throw the ball away," Thornton said. "I just jumped in front of him. I saw a couple of offensive linemen down the field, and I figured I could maneuver my way into the end zone."

Florida State went nowhere on its next possession, and the Bulldogs got the ball back at the FSU 37 after Damien Gary's 26-yard punt return. Richt surprised many when he put Shockley back into the game instead of starter David Greene.

On the first play, Shockley dropped back and threw a 37-yard touchdown to senior Terrence Edwards down the right sideline. Edwards wrestled the ball away from cornerback Stanford Samuels at the goal line for the 30th touchdown of his career, second-best in SEC history. Bennett's extra point gave the Bulldogs a 17-7 lead with 3:43 left in the half.

"After the fumble, I just told myself I was going to be more careful with the ball," Shockley said. "Coach

Richt came up to me on the sideline and said, 'You're going back in on the next series.' That gave me a lot of confidence, knowing that he still believed in me."

Said Richt: "D.J. made a great play, but he fumbled. I just wanted to make sure he knew that I believed in him, which I do. With D.J. in the game, I thought we had a much better chance of them playing single coverage because he is a running threat. I knew I wanted to go deep, and I felt if David went into the game, they would have played some zone coverages they'd been playing."

Florida State wasted a golden opportunity to score on its next possession when senior receiver Talman Gardner dropped what would have been a touchdown at Georgia's 5-yard line. The Seminoles were forced to punt, and the Bulldogs had a 17-7 lead at halftime.

On the opening possession of the second half, the Bulldogs rode Smith, who ran for 30 yards on four carries. Greene's 34-yard pass to Michael Johnson gave Georgia a first down at FSU's 29, but the Bulldogs

	1st	2nd	3rd	4th	Final
GEORGIA	3	14	6	3	26
FLORIDA STATE	0	7	6	0	13

SCORING SUMMARY

QTR	TEAM	PLAY	TIME
1st	**Georgia**	FG	Bennett 23-yd. field goal 4:19
2nd	**Florida St.**	TD	Boldin 5-yd. pass from Walker (Beitia kick) 13:41
2nd	**Georgia**	TD	Thornton 71-yd. interception return (Bennett kick) 6:24
2nd	**Georgia**	TD	Edwards 37-yd. pass from Shockley (Bennett kick) 3:43
3rd	**Georgia**	FG	Bennett 42-yd. field goal 11:06
3rd	**Georgia**	FG	Bennett 25-yd. field goal 8:49
3rd	**Florida St.**	TD	Thorpe 40-yd, pass from Boldin (run failed) 0:00
4th	**Georgia**	FG	Bennett 35-yd. field goal 10:17

OFFENSE

GEORGIA

PASSING	ATT	COMP	INT	YDS	TD
Greene	14	9	0	88	1
Shockley	7	3	0	37	0

RECEIVING	CATCHES	YDS	TD
Edwards	3	60	1
Gibson	2	12	0
Johnson	1	34	0
Brown	1	11	0
Watson	1	5	0
Wall	1	3	0
Smith	1	0	0

RUSHING	RUSHES	YDS	TD
Smith	23	145	0
Milton	5	13	0
Shockley	3	2	0
Wall	1	0	0
Greene	2	-7	00

FLORIDA STATE

PASSING	ATT	COMP	INT	YDS	TD
Boldin	14	6	0	78	1
Walker	12	7	2	69	1

RECEIVING	CATCHES	YDS	TD
Maddox	4	24	0
Boldin	3	34	1
Sam	2	11	0
Thorpe	1	40	1
Morgan	1	18	0
Hughes	1	14	0
Gardner	1	6	0

RUSHING	RUSHES	YDS	TD
Washington	10	48	0
Boldin	13	34	0
Maddox	9	32	0
Dean	1	5	0
Reid	1	2	0
Walker	7	-6	0

ABOVE:

Fans will be thrilled if the Bulldogs win the Sugar Bowl next season because it will mean they are national champions.
Brant Sanderlin/AJC

settled for Bennett's 42-yard field goal, which gave them a 20-7 lead with 11:06 left in the third quarter.

Georgia got another field goal after sophomore defensive end Will Thompson sacked Walker on the Seminoles' next play, forcing him to fumble. Defensive tackle Ken Veal recovered the ball at FSU's 17, and Bennett kicked a 25-yard field goal four plays later for a 23-7 lead.

The Bulldogs threw a season-low 15 passes and relied on their defense to stop the Seminoles. Georgia sacked FSU quarterbacks six times, and the Seminoles ran for 115 yards on 41 attempts. Walker was forced into action after Rix overslept an exam and backup quarterback Adrian McPherson was kicked off the team. Walker completed 7 of 12 passes for 69 yards, threw two interceptions and lost a fumble.

"When your defense is playing good and your kicking game is so solid, it can get kind of boring," Richt said. "But winning is fun."

The Seminoles pulled within 23-13 on the last play of the third quarter. Boldin threw a 40-yard touchdown to receiver Craphonso Thorpe down the right sideline. Boldin tried to run around right end for a two-point conversion, but linebacker Chris Clemons knocked him out of bounds at the 2-yard line. It wasn't enough.

Georgia got another field goal from Bennett on its next drive, and the celebration was on.

"Thirteen victories have never happened before," said Richt, whose second Georgia team produced the school's first Sugar Bowl victory since the 1980 season, when Vince Dooley's Dogs beat Notre Dame to win the national championship. "I'm sure Coach Dooley would've had 14 victories if he'd played 14 games. But we'll take it. We made history."

And the Bulldogs started making their plans for the 2004 Sugar Bowl, where the national championship will be decided.

"We'll have to start all over," Richt said. "We'll celebrate and enjoy this, but next year, we'll have to start all over."

> ## "IT'S THE KIND OF SEASON WHERE YOU'RE GLAD IT'S OVER. I'M GLAD IT'S OVER. "
>
> — FLORIDA STATE COACH BOBBY BOWDEN

ABOVE:
"I'd just as soon not play Coach Bowden again, unless it's next year, right here,"
Mark Richt said after defeating his mentor, Bobby Bowden. Brant Sanderlin/AJC

ABOVE:
Anquan Boldin caught Florida State's only touchdown
of the first half. He passed for the Seminoles' other touchdown,
which came with no time left in the third quarter.
Brant Sanderlin/AJC

RIGHT:
Musa Smith was Sugar Bowl MVP with
145 yards rushing on 23 carries.
Michael McCarter/AJC

" _IT WAS A GLORIOUS SEASON AND IT'S A BIG STEP. IN THE LOCKER ROOM, WE WERE HAPPY, BUT WE DIDN'T ACT LIKE IT'S THE FIRST TIME WE'VE WON A BIG GAME. THE PLAYERS ARE LEARNING HOW TO WIN, EXPECTING TO WIN. THAT'S A GREAT SIGN._ "

— BULLDOGS COACH MARK RICHT

ABOVE:
*David Greene finished the season with 2,924 passing yards,
the third-best season in Georgia history behind Eric Zeier in
1993 and 1994.*
Brant Sanderlin/AJC

RIGHT:
*Mark Richt received the obligatory ice
water shower after leading the Bulldogs
to their first 13-victory season.*
Brant Sanderlin/AJC

" THIRTEEN VICTORIES HAVE NEVER HAPPENED BEFORE. I'M SURE COACH DOOLEY WOULD'VE HAD 14 VICTORIES IF HE'D PLAYED 14 GAMES. BUT WE'LL TAKE IT. WE MADE HISTORY. "

— BULLDOGS COACH MARK RICHT

ABOVE:

Musa Smith, picking out his championship shirt, ran for 30 yards on four carries on the Bulldogs' opening possession of the second half. Michael McCarter/AJC

RIGHT:

As usual, UGA VI was there to support his team. Brant Sanderlin/Staff

ABOVE:
Mark Richt shared the Sugar Bowl trophy with Bobby Bowden before the game, but it was all Richt's when the game was over. *Brant Sanderlin/AJC*

BULLDOGS' REGULAR-SEASON STATISTICS

OFFENSE

PASSING

PLAYER	ATT	COMP	INT	PCT	YDS	TD
David Greene	336	192	8	57.1	2,599	21
D.J. Shockley	47	29	2	61.7	358	4
Cory Phillips	11	6	0	54.5	92	1
Terrence Edwards	1	1	0	100.0	4	0

RECEIVING

PLAYER	ATT	YDS	TD
Terrence Edwards	49	852	10
Fred Gibson	36	653	4
Benjamin Watson	29	316	2
Michael Johnson	27	339	2
Damien Gary	27	254	4
Reggie Brown	19	256	2
Musa Smith	13	108	0
Tony Milton	8	25	0
J.T. Wall	7	59	2
Bryan McClendon	5	90	0
Mario Raley	3	43	0
Tyson Browning	3	29	0
Gabe Galt	1	25	0
D.J. Shockley	1	4	0

RUSHING

PLAYER	ATT	YDS	TD
Musa Smith	218	1,073	6
Tony Milton	69	295	0
J.T. Wall	27	147	3
Tyson Browning	21	108	1
D.J. Shockley	32	108	2
Ronnie Powell	11	28	1
Braxton Snyder	3	5	0
Jeremy Thomas	4	4	0
Reggie Brown	1	3	0
Jon Stinchcomb	0	1	1
Cory Phillips	1	-6	0
Fred Gibson	1	-6	0
David Greene	59	-62	2

SPECIAL TEAMS

FIELD GOALS

PLAYER	1-19	20-29	30-39	40-49	50+
Billy Bennett	0/0	5/5	5/8	9/11	0/1

PUNTING

PLAYER	NO	AVG	INSIDE 20
Jonathan Kilgo	57	41.7	12

PUNT RETURNS

PLAYER	NO	YDS	AVG	TD
Damien Gary	27	410	15.2	1
Sean Jones	10	160	16.0	0
Terrence Edwards	2	40	20.0	0
Thomas Davis	1	18	18.0	0
David Pollack	1	16	16.0	0
Reggie Brown	1	25	25.0	0
Bruce Thornton	0	12	0.0	1

KICKOFF RETURNS

PLAYER	NO	YDS	AVG	TD
Fred Gibson	16	407	25.4	1
Terrence Edwards	13	202	15.5	0
Tim Jennings	5	97	19.4	0
Jarrett Berry	1	5	5.0	0

DEFENSE

TACKLES

PLAYER	SOLO	AST	TOTAL
Boss Bailey	57	46	103
Tony Gilbert	64	32	96
David Pollack	53	39	92
Sean Jones	35	48	83
Johnathan Sullivan	37	32	69
Kentrell Curry	26	38	64
Thomas Davis	35	20	55
Will Thompson	27	25	52
Chris Clemons	21	23	44
Greg Blue	24	18	42
Bruce Thornton	20	18	38

TACKLES

PLAYER	SOLO	AST	TOTAL	PLAYER	SOLO	AST	TOTAL
Decory Bryant	23	14	37	DeMario Minter	10	9	19
Tony Taylor	18	17	35	Arnold Harrison	7	11	18
Ken Veal	9	24	33	Derrick Holloway	12	6	18
Darrius Swain	19	14	33	Burt Jones	13	4	17
Kedric Golston	10	20	30	Derrick White	5	9	14
Robert Geathers	13	16	29	Jamario Smith	6	5	11
Ryan Davis	19	9	28	Kenny Bailey	8	1	9
Tim Jennings	13	14	27	Darrell Holmes	3	1	4
Gerald Anderson	9	15	24	Brandon Williams	0	3	3
Shedrick Wynn	11	8	19	Nic Clemons	0	1	1
				Jarod Noblet	0	1	1

SACKS

PLAYER	NO
David Pollack	12.0
Shedrick Wynn	4.5
Will Thompson	4.0
Boss Bailey	4.0
Johnathan Sullivan	3.0
Tony Gilbert	2.5
Robert Geathers	2.0
Thomas Davis	1.0
Chris Clemons	1.0
Kedric Golston	0.5
Arnold Harrison	0.5

INTERCEPTIONS

PLAYER	NO	YDS	AVG	TD
Kentrell Curry	3	139	46.3	1
Tim Jennings	3	109	36.3	1
Sean Jones	2	58	29.0	0
David Pollack	2	39	19.5	1
Thomas Davis	1	11	11.0	0
Darrius Swain	1	0	0.0	0
Bruce Thornton	1	0	0.0	0
Decory Bryant	1	0	0.0	0

TEAM

	GEORGIA	OPPOSITION
Scoring	394	196
Points per game	32.8	16.3
Touchdowns	48	26
First downs	253	212
Rushing	98	92
Passing	139	103
Penalty	16	17
Net yards rushing	1,679	1,416
Net yards passing	3,053	2,432
FGM/FGA	19/25	6/16

The Atlanta Journal-Constitution
ajc.com

The entire staff of *The Atlanta Journal-Constitution* contributed to the coverage of the 2002 University of Georgia's SEC championship season. We gratefully acknowledge the efforts of the Photography and Sports Departments.

Reporters
Mark Schlabach, Tony Barnhart, Curtis Bunn, Carlos Frias, Michelle Hiskey, John Hollis, Michael Lee, Al Levine, David Markiewicz, John Manasso, Wendy Parker, Carroll Rogers, Karen Rosen, Jeff Schultz, Mike Tierney, Jack Wilkinson

Columnists
Furman Bisher, Mark Bradley, Steve Hummer, Tim Tucker

Editors
Mike Knobler, Chip Towers, Robert Mashburn, Robbyn Footlick, Don Boykin, David Tulis, Celine Bufkin, Chris Hunt, John Glenn

Photographers
Brant Sanderlin, Michael McCarter, W.A. Bridges Jr., Rich Addicks, David Tulis, Jenni Girtman, Laura Noel

Copy Editors
Karen Park, Gerry Overton, Rick Zabell, George Leite, Clark Freeman, Mike Luck, Lisa Transiskus, Lisa Brown, Terry Doherty

Designers
Paul Kasko, Charlie Noell, Pat Fox, Alexis Stevens, Chris Tabakian

Image Archivists, Information Services
Kathy Drewke, Robert Cauvel, Valerie Lyons